KANGA:

THE CLOTH THAT SPEAKS

Sharifa M. Zawawi

AZANIYA HILLS PRESS

Published by

 AZANIYA HILLS PRESS

8 Fordham Hill Oval, 15C
The Bronx, NY 10468

in association with

AfricaRUs MultiMedia

23 Hampshire Drive
Plainsboro, NJ 08536
Tel: 609-7167224 Fax: 609-167015
Email: Africarus@aol.com

Kanga: The Cloth that Speaks
Copyright © 2005 Sharifa M. Zawawi

Cover Concept: Sharifa M. Zawawi
Book Design and Layout: 'Damola Ifaturoti
Cover Design: Dotun Olukoya

All requests for permission, and inquiries regarding rights should be mailed to
Azaniya Hills Press
8 Fordham Hill Oval 15-C
The Bronx, NY 10468

Library of Congress Control Number: 2005923329

ISBN: 0976694107

To the Memory of Miriam Drabkin

Colleague and Friend

ACKNOWLEDGEMENTS

I could not have written this book had it not been for the encouragement and support of many people. I was fortunate to find friends in New York, Oman and Zanzibar who were interested in what *kangas* say. Some collected kanga messages for me and some allowed me to study their own kanga collections. I should not forget those who let me read their *kangas* from their backs, those who allowed me to use their photographs and Eduardo J. Hernendez of The City University of New York who helped with their arrangement. My special gratitude goes to 'Damola Ifaturoti, my editor, who devoted scholarly effort and time formatting the book.

I am also greatly indebted to my friends Dr. Joan Vincent of Barnard College, Columbia University and Dr. Edgar Gregersen of Queen's College of The City University of New York. I would like to express my deepest appreciation to them for giving up precious time to read and comment on earlier drafts in the midst of working on their own manuscripts. Any errors and omissions are mine.

CONTENTS

ACKNOWLEDGEMENTS iv

INTRODUCTION vii

Myths of Custom and Origin vii

Research Procedures ix

CHAPTER ONE: SWAHILI CONTACT AND CULTURAL TRADITION 1

The Waswahili of the Diaspora 1

Movements and Settlements of People 2

Cultural Tradition, Contact and Change 3

CHAPTER TWO: THE ORIGIN OF THE KANGA AMONG THE WASWAHILI 5

Beginnings 5

Nineteenth Century Accounts 8

Glossaries, Dictionaries and Travelers' Accounts 11

CHAPTER THREE: KANGA MOTIFS, NAMES AND FASHIONS 19

Kanga Designs and Colors 19

Kanga Majina Names 20

Kanga Fashion and Good Taste 24

CHAPTER FOUR: THE IMPORTANCE OF KANGA 27

From Birth to Death 27

Production and Marketing 28

CHAPTER FIVE: KANGA MESSAGES 31

CATEGORIES OF MESSAGES

Friendship, Love, and Marriage 32

Hostility and Resentment 37

Family Relationships 40

Wealth and Strength, Cooperation and Competition 44

Patience, Tolerance and Faith 48

Experience, Knowledge and Action 53

Kindness and Generosity 55

Idd Greetings 57

Politics and National Identity 59

MESSAGES STRENGTHEN SOCIO-CULTURAL VALUES 75

PHOTOGRAPHS 61

CHAPTER SIX: KANGA LANGUAGE AND LITERARY TRADITION 77

Innovations 82

CONCLUSION 85

APPENDIX: KANGA TEXTS COLLECTED 1984-2001 87

KANGA NAMES AND THEIR DISTRIBUTION 123

MAP OF THE REGION 124

REFERENCES 125

INDEXES 127

FIGURES

1.	*Kisutu*	61
2.	Swahili 19-Century woman wearing a dress made out of a Kanga.	61
3.	*Kukopa furaha kulipa matanga* (in Arabic script)	61
4.	*Wema hauozi*	61
5.	Julius Nyerere 1922-1999	62
6.	*Jogoo* ZNP symbol	62
7.	UN Decade for women	62
8.	*Salama Salimina*	62
9.	*AlHamdulillah Àssalaama*	63
10.	Oman Coffee Pot	63
11.	*Kanga* at Darajani Street	63
12.	*Tumeamua*	63
13.	Women wearing *Kangas* at a shower party in Boston	64
14.	A Zanzibar child wearing *Kangas*	64
15 - 16.	Two styles in wearing a pair of *Kanga*	64
17.	*Kanga* worn as a headdress	65
18.	Three Zanzibar women in their *Kangas*	65
19.	*Mwaka* Celebration	65
20.	In Comoro *kanga* worn as saluva	65
21.	Oman National Day	66
22.	*Si mzizi*	66
23.	*Mapenzi hayafi*	66
24.	*Siri ya Mtungi*	67
25.	*Sifa ya mume*	67
26.	*Kanga bubu*	67
27.	*Kanga bubu*	68
28.	*Kanga bubu*	68
29.	*Mungu nijaalie*	69
30.	*Akufaaye ndiye rafiki*	69
31.	*Eid Mubarak*	70
32.	*Eid Mubarak*	70
33.	*Sikilizana na wenzio*	71
34.	A mutilated *Kanga*	71
35.	Hello Good morning	72
36.	*Akili ni mali*	72
37.	*Nadiymu-1-qalb*	73
38.	Fort Nakhl	73
39.	*Oman al-yawm*	74
40.	An Omani dress with *l-Haaf*	74

INTRODUCTION

Kikulacho kimo maungoni mwako
What consumes you is around your body

Culture, history, fashion and language are inextricably interwoven in this study of East African dress. In the simplest material sense, *Kangas* are nothing but two rectangles of cotton cloth, one worn as a dress fastened above the breasts, the other as a headdress and shawl covering the shoulders. Nevertheless, they mark the history of people; with changes in time there are new labels, new patterns and new messages.

The cultural significance of the *kanga* lies in the message it bears. In Swahili these are called *majina* which means literally 'names.' *Kanga* is a Swahili word referring to an item of clothing worn daily by ordinary Swahili speaking people, women and men, young and old. On the one hand, the *kanga* provides a practical, attractive, comfortable form of dress for a tropical climate; on the other hand, it is a century's old communicative device. The *kanga* cuts across gender and generation. All can wear it. More importantly, all can read its message. *Kangas* communicate: hence, "The Cloth that Speaks." *Kangas* communicate Swahili cultural and human values. As material and verbal art they maintain Swahili literary traditions and enrich them. They are a powerful means of expressing opinions— both personal and political— adding greatly to Swahili literature and oral tradition. *Kangas* are written and verbal discourses.

Myths of Custom and Origin

As an item of dress, the *kanga* is now ubiquitous in the countries around the Indian Ocean although its origins appear to lie along the shoreline – the *sahil* – of the African coast. Yet do they? That is one of the many questions this book seeks to answer.

Several myths surround the *kanga:*

√ that the messages that appear on *kangas* are by and large a female form of communication about matters that should not or cannot be spoken about openly.

√ that *kangas* are essentially associated with a woman's body, feminism and sexuality.

√ that *kangas* are mainly bought by men for their wives or girl-friends but are tabooed as gifts to relatives.

√ that *kangas* were first called *leso* (in Portuguese *lenço)* meaning the handkerchief squares that traders originally brought to East Africa in the sixteenth century.

√ that early *kanga* designs showed a pattern of white spots on a dark background and it was this that led buyers to call it *"kanga",* a Swahili word meaning a guinea-fowl with its spotty plumage.

√ that *kanga* developed in the nineteenth century and were worn in Mombasa in the 1860s and in Zanzibar in 1875.

These myths have grown up as today's Swahili scholars read the work of historians and ethnologists of the early twentieth century and unquestioningly accept their statements.[1] In this book, I use the Swahili language and Swahili literature to refute them.

The *kanga* has been wrongly associated exclusively with married life and adult sexuality. It is not true that "A man will only accept a kanga from a woman with whom a sexual relationship is possible never from mother or sister."[2]   Many gifts of *kangas* have been received by mothers from their sons and by sisters from their brothers and vice versa. Such an exchange of *kangas* is neither tabooed nor prohibited. *Kangas* serve as useful and inexpensive gifts for friends and relatives during times of happiness or sadness. As a guest a Swahili person carries a pair of *kangas* rather than chocolates, wine or flowers.

Several dubious explanations as to the origin of the word *kanga* have been put forward by writers who have based their interpretations on second-hand information and some rather Eurocentric views. The assertion that the word *leso* is borrowed from Portuguese would appear to have originated with Bernhard Krumm's book *Words of Oriental Origin in Swahili,* published in1940.[3] Some derive the word *kanga* from a guinea-fowl because of its spots and relate *leso* etymologically to Portuguese trade with the East African coast. H.P. Blok repeated the myth in 1948 in his *A Swahili Anthology.*[4] It then became part of a twentieth century European tradition that any African language development and culture was non-indigenous. Many others have repeated this assertation. Can the Portuguese not have acquired the word *leso* (*lenço*) for a handkerchief from the Swahili rather than the other way around?

Another usage of the word *kanga* refers to a guinea-fowl. This is a homonym and not an extension of meaning to *kanga* the cloth. These words of the same spelling and pronunciation are not related. They have different meanings and derivations. They are not synonyms with *kanga* as some scholars have claimed.[5] Early twentieth century writers who have made this connection include Harold Ingrams an officer in the Colonial Administrative services in Zanzibar in 1919. In his book *Arabia and the Isles,* he writes:

> Kangas were originally so-called because they were gray and spotted white
> like a guinea-fowl, for kanga also means guinea–fowl. Nevertheless, days
> when they were as plain as that had long since passed, and among the
> Swahilis all sorts of extraordinary patterns had their brief mode[6] .

An earlier suggestion that the word *kanga* meant a guninea-fowl appears in H.P. Blok, *A Swahili Anthology.* He identifies *kanga* as a guinea-fowl, citing M.Meinhof's, *Lautlehre der Bantu Sprachen,*1910. However, Blok does not include *kanga* to mean cloth in his glossary.[7]

What these writers failed to appreciate is that the trade in cloth and clothing occurred within the much wider context of the Indian Ocean over a much longer period. The Portuguese arrived in East Africa in the fifteenth century and had settlements on the coast from 1498 to 1698.[8] But long before their exploitation of East Africa, Arab travelers had written of the civilization that flourished in cities along the coast.

My analysis will correct these long-standing hypotheses and assumptions. The history of *kanga* did not start five centuries ago with the coming of the Portuguese to East Africa nor with the beginning of European trade. The Azaniya coast of East Africa played a significant role in the global trade and a rich material culture existed long before the introduction of western ideas and commodities to the region. As early as the 1830's one American traveler, Captain W.F.W. Owen, recalled and lamented the lost legacies of that ancient civilization "the devastation that the monopolizing spirit of mankind has produced on the east coast of Africa".[9]

Research Procedures: *Kanga* -The Cloth and the Message

My search for a better understanding of *kangas* led me to examine not only the history of *kangas* but their design, message and significance not only for Swahili speaking communities within the modern nations of East Africa and the Gulf states, but for those in the Swahili diaspora. *Kangas* are carriers of past and present Swahili attitudes and values. They reproduce, reaffirm and preserve Swahili cultural traditions.

In this complex, rapidly changing, modern world, it is rarely possible to know for certain the origin of any cultural features. Here, I take into account the complexity of *kanga* history and begin to trace anew the development of *kanga* as commodities from cloth to clothing, from u*nguo* to *kanga*. This leads me to follow the passages within an age-old mercantile system from Alexandria to the Sahil of East Africa and the further shores of the Indian Ocean, to Hadhramaut and Yemen, to the Gulf of Oman, and to India itself as well as, three centuries later, to the ports and manufacturing cities of Britain, Holland, China and Japan. The accounts of early travelers may permit us to trace the extension of the concept of '*kanga*' from simply a 'cloth' 'nguo' to a garment. Thereafter, the socio-cultural value of the *kanga* is related to the advent of modernity and change.

It is important to narrate *kanga's* historical existence through its evolution over specific time spans and within precisely delimited space and events. Thus I examine in chronological order travelers' tales and historical accounts—Greek, Arab, English and German—of where the cloth was to be found and the clothes that were made of it from the twelfth to the twenty first century, as well as changes that later occurred both in fashion and in nomenclature. Most helpful, in my search were the dictionaries and word lists in which, as strangers to a foreign land, Europeans recorded their observations of the different clothes that people wore—that most striking yet most common place feature of cross-cultural contact. To do this accurately, they were obliged to ask what this or that garment was called, and so they came to compile a dictionary of Swahili fashion. Sometimes, of course, they were wrong in their transcriptions of what they heard and sometimes they misheard. Regrettably, it was this that led later scholars into misunderstanding, misinterpreting and misrepresenting the complex history of *kanga* cloth and its evolution as an item of clothing.

I also explore oral tradition—especially children's rhymes and verses. As a child growing up in Zanzibar, I spent my afternoons playing with children from our home and the neighborhood. Other children joined us and were always welcomed. Many of our games were based on traditional rhymes chanted or sung. We, as children, did not know their meanings, their composers, their origin or their historical significance. These specifics were not of our concern but the songs preserved language and content. Later in this book, I discuss one of these rhymes in relation to the history of *kanga*.

Most important of all, however, are the *kangas* themselves – the clothes that speak. Here, I draw on a treasury of designs and inscriptions that appear on *kangas* I have collected over the past two decades. There are over seven hundred and fifty of them and the number grows with every occasion for remembrance or celebration. Each new message they carry provide, for me, an ever-open window on Swahili history, customs, and ethical values.

I provide literal translations when translating *kanga* messages so readers may make their own interpretations of them. When translating from one language to another, in this case from Kiswahili to English, it is not always easy to find exact equivalents in structure, vocabulary or conceptualization. For instance, a third person pronoun in Kiswahili is genderless but in English is identified by 'he' or 'she'. To avoid the use of these pronouns or their gender-bias equivalents, I sometimes use the plural 'they'.

No translation would be adequate for every reader; a student of Kiswahili might gain from a literal translation, while a general reader might be satisfied with a good English equivalent. In some cases I have provided both a literal and a more colloquial English translation.

I wrote *Kanga: The Cloth and the Message in East Africa* in 1986. Several other scholars were writing about the various types of African clothing and its symbolic role. Much was also written on the role and function of clothes and textiles. This literature dealt with West African garments such as the Ghanaian *kente,* the Nigerian *adinkra* (or *aladire*), or the Fulani *kherka,* an equivalent of Swahili *kharqah* the *kanga.* Discussion was often of a broad and general nature. Only a few writers expressed a specific interest in Swahili *kanga.*[10]

Since the 1980's several articles on *kangas* as communicative media have appeared in periodicals and journals[11]. Jeanette Hanby and David Bygott published in 1985 a small book, *Kangas: 101 Uses* that is mainly of interest to tourists and of little help to those seeking to understand the significance of *kangas* to Swahili society and the extension of *kanga* usage as a result of culture-contact. Rose Marie Beck wrote her dissertation on the subject of *kangas*, but it is in German and unfortunately I have not been able to read it. A book in English is long over due. More recently, the interest in *kangas* and their messages has extended to the Internet in www.glcom.com/hassan.

This book extends my earlier study of both *kangas* as cloth and the social and historical significance they bear. I am saddened to read a recently manufactured *kanga* from Oman that asserts:

Kanga ni uzuri sio jina
What makes a *kanga* is its beauty and not its name

I disagree.

*   *   *   *

The proverb that heads this chapter is a *kanga* text.

Kikulacho kimo maungoni mwako
What consumes you is around your body

A variant of this message is:

Kikulacho kimo nguoni mwako
What consumes you is in your garment

Nguoni means 'inside the clothes of the wearer'and *maungoni* means 'around the body.' Clothes reveal what is close to the wearer. Not only do they protect or expose, enhance or impair; they also express the social or psychological dimensions of the personalities they serve. Thus, besides its practical utility, the purpose of a Swahili *kanga* is to communicate with others through the written message it bears.

Kanga: The Cloth and the Message was first presented and discussed at an African Studies Association conference held in Detroit, U.S.A. in 1987. For that conference, I examined 112 messages inscribed on *kangas* that I had collected over a period of three years from 1984 to 1987

Five years later on October 27, 1992, I presented an expanded version of that talk to students at Columbia University. This was based on even more 'names'. Over time my interest has grown even more. *Kanga*: The Cloth that Speaks continues my exploration of *kanga as* communicative artifact that nurtures and nourishes a culture. It discusses 750 *kangas* that appear with a message, extracting and analyzing their meaning and context. It also discusses 50 *kangas* that do not speak. These are known as *kanga bubu, kangas* that do not speak. They are without messages.

Kanga texts or messages are an important way of learning about the Swahili heritage, its past and its present cultural values. The messages printed on the cloth are permanent — yet of their time. Read and studied over time (as I have done) *kangas* provide a source for the study of aesthetics, history and that branch of philosophy that deals with ethics, a set of moral principles. Thus I set out to answer the question: What do these *kangas* say and to whom do they speak?

I divide the book into six chapters together with a Conclusion and an Index of the 750 *kanga* texts. They show how Swahili society's attitudes and views evolved with time and over space extending throughout several diasporas to show the wide range of social intercourse that *kangas* embrace. These extend through East Africa, across the Indian Ocean, to Europe and its centers of learning and to the United States; a global world that we now read about in modern Swahili novels.

The Swahili messages fall into nine categories.

> Friendship, Love, and Marriage
> Hostility and Resentment
> Family Relationships
> Wealth and Strength, Cooperation and Competition
> Patience, Tolerance and Faith
> Experience, Knowledge and Action
> Kindness and Generosity
> Idd Greetings and Festivity[12]
> Politics and National Identity

Kanga the Cloth that Speaks is not only for linguists, cultural anthropologists and historians interested in Eastern Africa, the Arabian Gulf and other regions of the Indian Ocean. It is also for the general reader concerned with the significance of clothing and inscriptions in the development of a society and culture and for all who are interested in the Swahili Diaspora worldwide. Finally, students of Swahili language and culture will find in it an invaluable supplement to their language textbooks. It is my hope that in all these areas, it may stimulate research, discussion and enjoyment.

Notes

1. Laura Fair, *Pastimes and Politics* (Ohio, 2001) 68, 78-81.
2. Farouque Abdillahi and Gill Shepherd, "I am like a kanga-cloth. I die in all my beauty," *Africa Now*, February 1984, 49.
3. Bernhard Krumm, *Words of Oriental Origin in Swahili* (London, 1940) 167.
4. H. P. Blok, *A Swahili Anthology* (London,1948)177.
5. Numerous others since Ingrams have connected *kanga* with a guinea-fowl. One of them is Julia Hilgar, "The Kanga: An Example of East African Textile Design", Picton et al, *The Art of African Textiles Technology, Tradition and Lurex* (London, 1979) 5.
6. See page 33.
7. Ibid. 170.
8. Sir John Gray, *History of Zanzibar from the Middle Ages to 1856* (London, 1962) 31.

9. W.F.W. Owen, *Narrative of Voyages to explore the shores of Africa Arabia and Madagascar* Robinson, Heaton Bowstead (ed.), (New York, 1833) 33.

10. Abdillah and Shapherd 1984, 48-49. In the same issue Fatma Shaaban Abbdullah published "Reflection on a Symbol", 49-50.

11. Abdillah and Shapherd 1984, Abdullah1984, Hilal 1989, Linnebuhr 1992, Hongoke 1993, Yahya-Othman 1995 and 1997, Beck 1997 and 2000, and as a chapter in a book (Hilgar, 1995).

12. Eid or Idd is a Muslim celebration that takes place after the fasting month of Ramadhan or after the pilgrimage to Mecca.

CHAPTER ONE
SWAHILI CONTACT AND CULTURAL TRADITION

I divide this chapter into three parts. First, I identify the Waswahili people. Second, I discuss their dispersion and the spread of their language. Finally, I examine *kangas* as cultural tradition of contact and change.

I define a Mswahili as a person of any ethnic or racial group who speaks Swahili as a first language. As a people, the Waswahili are heterogeneous in their ethnic composition but homogeneous in their religion, culture and language. They consist of speakers of various dialects of Swahili who understand each others' dialect.

The Waswahili of the Diaspora

Historically Waswahili have been variously defined (or on occasion have defined themselves) as, Waafrika (people of Africa), Wazanzibari (people of Zanzibar), Wangazija (people of Ngazija, i.e. the Comoro Islands), Waarabu (Zanzibar Arabs i.e. people from Arabia), Washihiri (people of ShiHir in Hadhramaut), Wamvita (people of Mvita i.e. Mombasa), Waamu (people of Lamu), Wapemba (people of Pemba), WaTanzania (people of Tanzania), and WaKenya (people of Kenya). The cosmopolitan heartland of the Waswahili stretches from the south Somali coast to Mozambique and includes the Zanzibar archipelago.

Besides Waarabu another term now is in use for people from Arabia. This identifies the Arabs of the Diaspora, Wamanga. Most have come from Oman[1] but the term is sometimes applied to Arabia in general. In 1920 Major F.B. Pearce, the British Resident in Zanzibar, in his account of the population of the Island Metropolis of Eastern Africa distinguishes four different categories of Arab resident. These are:

1. Mshihiri Arabs from the Hadramaut
2. Comorian Arabs from the Comoro Islands
3. Shatri, Mafazi, and Coast Arabs
4. Oman Arabs[2]

Although Pearce does not use -*manga* in his account, Richard Burton mentioned the term in his account of Zanzibar.[3] Frederick Johnson in *A Standard Swahili-English Dictionary* (1939) defines Manga as:

> "n. a name of Arabia, esp. the region of Muscat in the Persian Gulf. It is used to describe various objects connected with or derived from Arabia e.g. *pilipili manga*, black pepper. *mkomamanga*, pomegranate tree. *njiwa*

manga, a variety of pigeon. Johnson derives the term *manga* from the Arabic *manqa'* the sea.[4]"

I suggest that the more likely derivation of *manga* is *manqal* with the root *-naql* movement that it refers to ' people who have emigrated from a place'. Thus *wa-manga<wa-manqal < -naqal* "move from lodging" and *manqala* "a journey, a movement" i.e. emigrants. This term may be related to *magan* a word found in ancient inscriptions now considered Oman.

Movements and Settlements of People

The oldest and probably largest movement of people within the Swahili Diaspora crisscrossed the Azania/ Azaniya (coast), the Zingium,[5] the ocean that extends from the north of the Arabian Gulf [Red Sea] to the Cape of Good Hope at the southern tip of Africa. This is first mentioned in *The Periplus of the Erythrean Sea (106 A.D.),* an account of trade from the Red Sea and the coast of Africa to the East Indies at a time when Egypt was a province of the Roman Empire. 'Erythrean' is the name given by the unknown author to the whole expanse of ocean reaching from the coast of Africa to the utmost boundary of ancient knowledge in the east.

Beyond the African shoreline lies the 'continent of Azania'. The *Periplus* describes the coast of Azania from Cape Aromata to Rhapta. The name *Azania* is said to be derived from an Arabic phrase "Barr el-Khazain", the Land of Treasures, *barr* meaning land, *al-* the definite article and *khazain* the plural of *khaziyna* "treasure". Burton in his book *Zanzibar, City, Island an Coast*, wrongly translates this phrase as 'The Land of Tanks [6]. The author of *Periplus* reports that the Arabians were the first navigators of the Indian Ocean, and the first transporters of Indian produce. Thus trade connections between Arabia and East Africa were already established in the first century A.D.

George Fadlo Hourani, an Arab scholar, examined documentary evidence of these contacts in his book *Arab Seafaring.* He writes:

> Sumerian and Akkadian inscriptions of the third millennium B.C. report maritime relations between Mesopotamia and the countries of Dilmun, Magan and Melukhkha. Dilmun is probably the island of al-Bahrayn. Magan is now generally agreed to be Oman, ... Melukhkha is regularly associated with Magan in the inscriptions but its location at this period cannot yet be more closely determined.... On the western side of Arabia, Egyptian vessels were sailing on the Red Sea from at least the reign of Sahure (c2470 B.C.) of the Fifth dynasty, and under the Sixth Dynasty (c2341-2181 B.C.) journeys were made quite frequently by land or by sea to the country of Punt, probably the Somali coast facing Arabia.[7]

The history of the East African coast is also recorded in local chronicles, the best known of which is the Kilwa Chronicle. Its anonymous author writes about the coming of Shirazi emigrants from Persia to the towns along the coast in A.D. 957. H. Neville Chittick, an archaeologist, has questioned this date[8] but vestiges of such contact are seen in the presence of Washirazi in Zanzibar and Pemba and the celebration of *Mwaka* or *Nairuz*, the Shirazi agricultural solar calendar of 365 days. I describe this celebration later in this book.

Over time, the Greeks of Egypt and the Romans also engaged in this trans-oceanic commerce.[9] Among the articles of trade were Egyptian cottons, clothes imported from Arake (Malabar) and Barygaza

(Gujerat). These made in the Arabian fashion, were muslin cloaks with sleeves, quilts and embroidered sashes of different shades.[10]

The contact of Oman with the coast of East Africa was documented by Ibn "Ali bin Al-Husayn ibn 'Ali Al-Mas'udi (890-956 A.D.) in his *Kitab Muruj al-Dhahab wa ma 'adinu al-Jawhar* written in 332 A.H. This was published in Cairo in 1303A.H. in the Islamic calendar; in the Christian calendar1885 A.D.[11] In his panoramic account of the world and its people, Mas'udi notes that maritime people, 'Umani, cross this channel to the island of Qanbaluw (i.e. Pemba) in the sea of Al-zunj.

Twentieth century western scholars including H. Neville Chittick, G.S.P. Freeman-Grenville, J.E.G. Sutton, Edward A. Alpers, John de Allen, Norman Bennett, and C.S. Nicholls have discussed the historical movements and settlements of people on the Swahili coasts. I examined and discussed these in my study *Contact and Change: A Sociolinguistic Study of the East African Coast* written in 1978[12]. Arab traders settled first on the East African coast and then moved inland as far as western Congo. They married local women and gave birth to Arab-African Swahili-speaking offspring. In brief, both the Omanis and the Waswahili were maritime peoples who met through trade, social and cultural contacts.

Kanga as Cultural Tradition of Contact and Change

Muscat and other Oman seaports were geographically well sited on this ancient trade route to enable them to gain commercial access eastwards to India, China and the coast and westwards to the islands of the east African coast including the large islands of Zanzibar, Comoro and Madagascar. These commercial movements transferred not only trade goods, but also religious, political and social customs and ways of life. The constant exchange of goods and ideas led to admixtures of people, culture and language. Movement involved sharing many cultural institutions and artifacts producing cultural diversity in form of dress, beliefs, rituals, customs, values, attitudes, music, and cuisine. The term 'culture' includes verbal and non-verbal expression. These contribute to a way of life and group identity of today's Waswahili and Omanis. Today *kanga* texts in both Swahili and Arabic testify to this long cultural history of centuries of contact and change. Descendants of the Arab-African speakers plus Omani rule of Mombasa, Zanzibar, Pemba and Dar es Salaam from the 19th century brought about long term residence and over 300 years of coming and going of family members between Gulf States and East Africa coastal regions not simply trade contacts.

Throughout the Gulf States—Oman, the United Arab Emirates, Kuweit and Qatar — the movements of people contributed to an amalgam and fusion of the region's many socio-cultural compositions. Arabic is the national language of the region but many immigrants from East and Central Africa speak Swahili as their first or second language and have spoken it for centuries. *Kangas* are among the leading artistic and cultural links between East Africa and Oman, as well as the other countries of the Gulf States. An elegant long dress with matching shawl is the popular attire of the women of the region and *kangas* are an essential component of their costume. More *kanga* designs are now printed for Oman stores than are produced and bought in East Africa, their historical homeland.

Today many different African groups speak Kiswahili as their first language, and are identified as Waswahili for this reason. Besides early Arab traders and settlers, European missionaries and colonial and post-colonial administrators all contributed to the spread of Kiswahili. Now large communities of Waswahili are to be found in Africa, the Arabian Gulf, India, China, Europe, Russia and the U.S. Indeed, throughout the globe.

Kangas are now widely worn not only by Waswahili living on the East African coast, for whom they are traditional garments, but by people in different parts of Central and Southern Africa, the Arabian Gulf States and even farther away in the west and east of the universe. In the U.S. women who have been to eastern Africa bring back with them *kangas* that they use as curtains for their windows, wall hangings, tablecloths or shawls. In recent years, *kangas* have been found on sale in the shops and street stalls of New York City from 81st Street and Lexington Avenue to Harlem, and in the grandest stores such as Macy's and Neiman Marcus. *Kangas* traveled with Swahili speakers and the language of messages written on them went with them.

In this book, I focus on *kangas* that travel to many parts of the Gulf States and East Africa as gifts to relatives and friends and on *kangas* sold in markets around the Indian Ocean. In particular, I illustrate and discuss *kangas* and their messages from Dar es Salaam, Mombasa, Zanzibar and Muscat.

Notes

1. 'Umaan (Oman) is said to be derived from the Arabic root *'aman* meaning to reside in a place and *'umaaniy* means a resident of Oman.
2. F.B. Pearce, *The Island Metropolis of Eastern Africa* (London, 1920) 215.
3. R.F. Burton, *Zanzibar, City, Island and Coast* (London, 1872) 61.
4. See F. Johnson, *A Standard Swahili-English Dictionary* (London, 1939).
5. This text is said to have been compiled in c.547 A.D. It was translated by J.W.McCrindle in 1897. This Christian Egyptian monk used the name Zingium to refer to the region stretching south of Egypt to the Equator. This term also applied the ocean that extends from the north of the Arabian Gulf to the Cape of Good Hope in the south of the African continent. See William Vincent, *The Periplus of the Erythrean Sea* (London, 1800) 137.
6. R.F. Burton refers to water tanks in *Zanzibar, Vol.* I (London, 1872) 20.
7. Hourani, George F., *Arab Seafaring* (Princeton, 1951) 31.
8. H.Neville Chittick,"The Shiraz Colonization of the East African Coast" (London, 1965) 275-294 establishes the date of their arrival as the second half of the twelfth century A.D.
9. W. Vincent, 2-3.
10. Ibid. 4.
11. A.H. stands for Al-Hijra, the migration of Prophet MuHammad from Mecca to Madina and is the first year of Islamic calendar. A.D. stands for the Latin expression Anno Domini, in the year of the Lord, symbolizing the birth of Christ.
12. This was an extension of *Loan Words and their Effect on the Classification of Swahili Nominals* (Zawawi, 1979).

CHAPTER TWO
THE ORIGIN OF KANGA AMONG THE WASWAHILI

Here I discuss the early appearance of the *kanga* cultural tradition, tracing its historical emergence through its language and literature. I draw the reader's attention to a rich civilization with an affluent class-structured urban society ranging from rulers, princesses and princes to the common people. My main focus is on the terms used for five types of garment: *nguo, kisutu, doti, leso* and *kanga* with which the *kanga* has been identified. The garment that is now known as *leso* in Oman and Mombasa and as *kanga* in Zanzibar was first called *nguo mbili*. The Waswahili wore this garment long before the introduction of the words *kanga* and *leso* into the Swahili language.[1]

Beginnings

We may never know the true origin of *kangas* because we are reliant solely on language and oral history for our knowledge of it. Nevertheless, words and their usage allow us to rediscover socio-cultural traditions that have been lost. They illuminate obscure and forgotten concepts. From a popular verse sung by Swahili children at play we learn that what today we know as *kangas* were once called *nguo mbili*, two cloths. It is sung in a children's handgame where a few children sit in a circle and pile their hands on top of each other's, singing a verse called the *Kinyuri* verse after which the child whose hand is on the top removes it followed by the child who's hand is next in pile. A child drops out of the game wherever both hands are removed.

The song runs as follows:

Kinyuri nyurika	Kinyuri be like kinyuri
Mwanangu mwana jumbe	My daughter is the daughter of a chief
*Kavaa **nguo mbili***	She is wearing **two cloths**
Ya tatu kajiambika[2]	She is carrying a third one
Mkakaa sina urembo	Desolate, I have no fine garments
Aliye juu na arushe.	The hand that is on top should be withdrawn from play.

The wearing of two cloths and the carrying of a third probably as protection from the sun goes back to time immemorial.

Sources for the use of the term *kanga* are more formal. They include early Arab travelers' accounts and, later, the published dictionaries and observations of European visitors to East Africa. In the twelfth century one Arab traveler to the coastal towns of BaHar al-hind (the Indian Ocean) was Abu 'Abdallah MuHammad bin MuHammad 'Abdallah bin Idris Al-Hamudi Al-Hasan better known as Shariff Al-Idris

(1100-1166). In his *Kitaab Nuzhat al-Mushtaaq fiy Ikhtiraaq al-afaaf*, [The recreation of he who yearns to traverse the lands] he describes the clothes worn by the people of the island of k-r-mah [Kama?] as consisting of a wrapper *al-uzur* and a shawl *alfuwTa*.[3] Here Shariff Al-Idris tells us of the wearing of **two pieces of cloths** by the residents of these towns of the Indian Ocean.

Some two hundred years later another traveler, Abu Abdullah Muhammad Ibn Ibrahim, better known as Ibn BaTTuTa (1304 -1377) wrote about the towns of the al-sawaHil [the coasts]. Ibn BaTTuTa was an African Arab from Tangier in North Africa. In his book *RiHlat, TuHfat al-NaZZar fiy Gharaaib al-amSaar wa 'ajaaib al-asfaar-* [The Wonders of Cities and the Marvels of Travels.] He marvels at the advanced civilization he finds on his travels. In his account of Mugadishu in Somalia, he reports that cloths made there are exported to Egypt and other countries. He describes men wearing silk wraps which they fasten around the waist and embroidered tunics made out of Egyptian cotton as well as embroidered Egyptian turbans. Here is a second reference to the two garments being worn above and below the waist. He tells us that such articles of clothing were presented as gifts by the local inhabitants to the captains and owners of trading vessels on their arrival in port. Later two types of cotton cloth used in Somalia were known as sinjibari (from Zanzibar) and mesketi (from Muscat in Oman).

After leaving Mugadishu Ibn BaTTuTa visited Aden, Zufaar and Oman. He described the clothes only of the people of Zufaar in Oman. This town is referred to in the ancient scriptures as the Ophir of King Solomon,[4] whose fleets were laden with gold, *almug* trees (a gum tree from *al-muql*)[5] and precious stones. Ibn BaTTuTa reports:

> Their clothes are made out of cotton and are imported from India. They tie a wrap around their waist in place of trousers and many of them tie another wrap around the waist, like a sash. They put another piece of cloth on their backs because of the strong sun. They wash many times a day. There are many mosques [in Zufaar] and in each mosque there are many places where people can wash. In this town they make very beautiful silk, cotton and linen cloth.[6]

Two centuries later at the beginning of the sixteenth century, a Portuguese traveler Duarte Barbosa provides further information on the coastal trade of East Africa and Malabar. He describes the Moors of Sofala:

> … they come to sea in small barks, which they call zanbucs [sambuks] from the kingdoms of Quiloa [Kilwa] and Mombaza [Mombasa] and Melindi [Malindi] and they bring much cotton cloth [some] of many colours [others] white and blue and some of silk and gray and red and yellow beads which come to the said kingdoms in other larger ships from the great kingdom of Cambay which merchandise these Moors buy and collect from other Moors.[7]

Barbosa adds:

> The Moors have now recently begun to produce much fine cotton in this country and they weave it into white stuff because they do not know how to dye it or because they have not got any colours; in addition, they take the blue or coloured stuffs of Cambay and unravel them and again weave these with their white threads and in this manner they make coloured stuffs by means of which they get much gold.[8]

The author then describes the inhabitants of Quiloa (Kilwa):

> These people are Moors of a dusky colour, and some of them are black and some white; they are very well dressed with rich cloths of gold and silk, and cotton, and the women also go very well dressed out with much gold and silver chains and bracelets on their arms, and legs and ears.[9]

Barbosa also describes Pemba, Manfia [Mafia] and Zanzibar. He writes:

> In the islands they live in great luxury and abundance; they dress in very good cloths of silk and cotton which they buy in Mombaza off the merchants from Cambay who reside there. Their wives adorn themselves with many jewels of gold from Sofala and silver in chains, earrings, and are dressed in silk stuffs.[10]

There is evidence, too, of extensive trade not simply between north and south along the Eastern African coast but further afield, around the shores of the Indian Ocean. Trade in cloth and in clothes between Oman and Azaniya is further confirmed by a letter written by Nasikha bint Su'uwd in Muscat to Sheikh Mwinyi Juma Kaja (Kwaja) of Zanzibar in the seventeenth century. The language is Swahili, the script Arabic.[11] Nasikha complains about the shortage of cloth:

Arabic script version: *Maskati kakuna jabu haku mata'a kakuna*
Modern Standard Swahili: *Maskati hakuna jambo huku vitu hakuna*
Literal English translation: Muscat nothing wrong here trade goods not available
Arabic script version: *mashaqqa katubati ghuwo kuvala shuqqa tubu*
Modern Standard Swahili: *mashaka hatupati n-guwo kuvaa shuka tupu.*[12]
Literal English translation: difficult we do not get cloths to wear wraps [piece of cloth] only

The passage translates in English thus:

> Muscat is fine [literally, there is no problem]; (but) there are no trade goods.
> This year there are no cloths for wearing; there are only plain wraps.

This letter is dated 1643. It shows that, at that time, two words were in use for 'cloth' in Swahili. These were *ghuwo* [*guwo/nguwo/nguo*] and *shuqqa*.

The two items of clothing that appear in this letter are *nguo* and *shuka*. The Swahili word *nguo* means clothes and the Arabic word shuqqah or *shuka* signifies part of a cloth, an oblong piece used as a wrap.

From these early documents we see first, a symbiotic relationship that exists between the northern and southern towns of the Swahili coast and Muscat in Oman. The similarities of culture that remain among them today vouches for long years of contact and an exchange of commodities and ideas that has taken place over centuries. Second, we see that cloth was not only to be found in Eastern Africa by the twelfth century but that some was actually produced there. Third, a form of dress consisting of two pieces of cloth with one worn as a wrap below the waist and the other as a shawl was to be found not only in Eastern Africa but in countries around the Indian Ocean. Several texts refer to the wearing of cloth, and in particular to the use of wrap and shawl by East Africans. However, the name *kanga* is not yet in use.

Nineteenth Century Accounts

The accounts of European travelers around the Indian Ocean also reveal early contacts and trade. Among the earliest nineteenth century writers is Henry Salt whose book *Voyage to Abyssinia and Travels into the interior of that Country in the years 1809 and 1810* was published in 1816. Given the dependence of the transoceanic trade upon the monsoon winds, we may be assured that his description would hold for earlier periods as well. Salt writes:

The common track pursued by the Arab traders is as follows:

> They depart from the Red Sea in August (before which it is dangerous to venture out of the Gulf) then proceed to Muscat and thence to the coast of Malabar. In December they cross over to the coast of Africa, visit Mugdasho, Marea, Brava, Lamo, Melinda and Querimbo islands; they then direct their course to the Comoro Islands and the northern ports of Madagascar or sometimes stretch down southward as far as Sofala. This occupies them till after April when they run up into the Red Sea where they arrive in time to refit and prepare a fresh cargo for the following year. This is the regular course of the trade.[13]

A few years later Captain W.F. Owen surveyed the whole coast line of Eastern Africa and the Arabian Gulf between 1822 and 1826. An account of his adventures appears in *Narratives of Voyages to Explore the Shores of Africa, Arabia and Madagascar*. He writes:

> It is really melancholy to contemplate the devastation that the monopolizing spirit of mankind has produced on the east coast of Africa. Wherever we went, even in the most obscure harbours, we could trace the remains of former wealth and civilization contrasted strongly with present poverty and barbarism.[14]

Nevertheless, reflecting on the conditions of the slaves in Mombasa, Owen writes favorably of their clothes:

> The condition of the slaves belonging to the Arabs of Mombasa is highly creditable to their humanity; they cannot always be distinguished from their masters, as they are allowed to imitate them in dress and in other particulars.[15]

This is an important comment since it suggests the likelihood of Arab-style dress spreading widely among the population at large. Owen describes the people of the Congo whom he also visited:

> … the prince… was accompanied by six of his daughters, who as specimens of the women on the coast, were rather superior. They were of large stature, well formed and with pleasing, intelligent countenances; they were dressed in gaudy-coloured cloths of English manufacture, secured round their waist, and hanging down to their ankles, a piece of the same stuff was also thrown carelessly over the shoulders so as to cover the bosom.[16]

Owen visited this region in 1822. His description of the garment worn by the Congo princesses is exactly that of *nguo mbili*, which as we have seen, later became known as **kisutu, doti, leso** *or* **kanga**. He also says, quite clearly that their garments were manufactured in England.

The distinguished explorer Richard F. Burton made a major contribution to the history of East African costume in 1860. In his famous account of his travels in Africa Burton depicts at some length the historical mercantile connections around the Indian Ocean. Burton reports that Zanzibar imported from Europe and America silks, cottons, chintzes, and calico. In 1863 American merchants who formerly sent 'domestics' from the Massachusetts Mills, because of the civil war, had to import Manchester goods. Imports from Great Britain reached Zanzibzr through India.[17] In the course of his account Burton verifies an indigenous Swahili interest in modes of dress.[18] Most intriguingly, he writes specifically of what the local people called "cloths with names."

They were picking up distinctions that were being made in the metropolitan.

> The cloths imported into East Africa are of three kinds, Merkani, Kaniki, and "cloths with names", "Merkani," in which we detect the African corruption of American, is the article "domestics"- unbleached shirting and sheeting from the mills near Salem.[19] Kaniki, is the common Indian indigo dyed cotton. "Cloths with names," as they are called by the Africans, are Arab and Indian checks, and coloured goods of cotton or silk mixed with cotton.[20]

Burton then distinguishes two kinds of "cloths with names":

> Of these, the most common is the *Barsati,* a dark blue cotton cloth with a broad red stripe, which, representing the dollar in the interior, is useful as presents to chiefs. Of double value is the *Dabwani* made at Maskat [Muscat], a small blue and white check, with a quarter breadth of red stripe, crossed with white and yellow: this showy article is invariably demanded by the more powerful Sultans for themselves and their wives whilst they divide the *Merkani* and *Kaniki,* which composes their *Honga* – "blackmail" or dash - amongst their followers.[21]

The trade names identify the quality of the cloth being passed on from the elite merchants, chiefs, princes and sultans to members of the population at large.

The cloth that Burton labels *Barsati* is still used in Oman and coastal East Africa in the making of *kilemba,* a turban worn by a government official. *Dabwani* appears as *debwani* in Johnson's dictionary to describe "a kind of loin-cloth, also a turban cloth; an Indian cloth, mostly of silk, with red or brown stripes, and worn on the head as a turban" He derives it from Persian *diba* brocade.[22] In Arabic the word is *dibaj* and meaning brocade.

Burton continues:

> In Eastern Africa, cotton cloth is used only for wear. The popular article is a piece of varying breadth but always of four cubits, or six feet, in length: the *braça* of Portuguese Africa. It is called by the Arabs *shukkah,* by the Wasawahili, *unguo,* and in the far interior *upande* or *lupande*. It is used as a loin-wrapper, and is probably the first costume [i.e. most widely worn] of Eastern Africa and of Arabia.[23]

All these terms—**shuka**, **nguo** and **upande**—still exist in the Swahili language. They relate to any type of wrap-around garments. The word *shuka* does not relate to a part of the body as it does in the English word loin-cloth. It stands for a piece of cloth of an oblong shape.

Burton goes on to say that the wearing of the *shukkah* as a national dress during the pilgrimage to Mecca proves its antiquity throughout the regions around the east of the Red Sea. He adds:

> On the African coast the *Shukkah Merkani* is worth about 0.25 dollars = 1s.0½d., in the interior it rises to the equivalent of a dollar (4s.2d.) and even higher. The *Kaniki* is but little cheaper than the *Merkani*, when purchased upon the sea-board; … A double twelve-foot length of *shukkah* an article worn by women who can afford it, is called a **Doti**, and corresponds with the **Tobe** [*thôb*] of Abyssinia and of the Somali. The whole piece of *Merkani*, which contains from seven to eleven *Doti*, is termed a Jurah or Gorah.[24]

Putting a price on a type of a cloth allows the evaluation of one as better than another.

The *thob* that Burton mentions closely resembles today's *kanga* but is larger. It is 70 inches long by 50 inches wide and consists of one long piece of cloth. He uses the word *doti* to describe a *shukkah* of four yards in length worn by women is combined to mean 'a pair' of as in today's taxonomy. The word *doti* is still in use in Swahili. Johnson describes doti as a piece of cloth suited for, and worn as, a loin-cloth, shuka, i.e. about 2 yards of full width, or 4 yards of narrow material." He derives it from Hindi `duhuwtiy'. In Tanzania *doti* refers to two pieces of cloth as in **Doti ya kanga,** a pair of *kanga*. **Gora ya leso** is the equivalent in Kenya.[25]

"The full length of *merkani*, which contains from seven to eleven *doti*, is termed a *jurah* or *gorah*." The word *jora* is said to be from the Hindi *juwr*, a length of calico about 30 yards in length. In Zanzibar *jora* was used to refer to any long piece of fabric which merchants cut into dress lengths for people to buy. In the Oman dialect of Arabic, the sound /j/ alternates with /g/ and so we see both *jora* and *gora* appearing in Swahili with two different meanings: *gora* the two pieces of the same length (as in *doti of kanga*) and *jora* one very long piece that comes in bale.[26]

Burton reports that cloth was made in East Africa. Men spun cotton on a *mlavi*, a spindle, and wove it on *utanda*, a loom frame. They also wove and dyed the cloth. Dyes were obtained from the juice of the *mzima* tree, the root of the *mdaa* a plant that produces a black dye and the leaves of red holcus. Good taste was shown in the designs.. they are sometimes checks with squares, alternately black and white, or in stripes of black variegated with red dyes upon a white ground: the lines are generally broad in the center, but narrow along the edges..

All cloths had a fringe, or *tamvua*. Despite the labour expended upon these cloths, the largest size may be purchased for six feet of American domestic (*Merkani*), or for a pair of iron hoes. There is therefore little inducement to extend their manufacture.[27]

Burton's "clothes with names" is a translation of a Swahili idiom "*nguo ya jina,*" The higher the quality of the cloth, the more likely it is that it will be given a name. A name bestows both meaning and worth; that which is without a name is meaningless and worthless.[28] Indeed, there is a *kanga* that affirms:

Jina jema hungara gizani
A beautiful name shines in the dark

Glossaries, Dictionaries and Travelers' accounts

From 1850 on, glossaries, dictionaries and travelers' accounts carry us even closer to the elusive *kanga*. In that year Johannes Ludwig Krapf, a German missionary for the Anglican Church Missionary Society who was stationed in Mombasa from 1844 - 1862, published his first Swahili dictionary. He translates all three English words cloth, dress and garment by one word *unguo* (*nguo*).[29] Krapf makes it clear that at that time the same word *unguo* meant both cloth and clothes in Swahili whereas today, in the twenty-first century, *nguo* signifies only clothes and the Swahili word for cloth is *kitambaa*. Other garments Krapf names at this time are:

shirt	*kansu[kanzu]*
trousert [trousers]	*suruali*

Kanzu is not a shirt but a long, wide robe-like garment worn by both men and women. It is called *qanbaaz* or *dishdasha* in Arabic - *Sirwaal or surwal* in Persian, Hindi and Arabic means trousers. Krapf provides no other terms for clothes. There is no *nguo mbili* no *kanga*.

In 1865, Bishop Edward Steere of the Anglican Universities Mission to Central Africa (UMCA) was posted to Zanzibar. He immediately began to compile a *Handbook of the Swahili Language* on which he worked from July 1865 to 1870. In a description of costumes in Zanzibar, he reports:

> Slaves and very poor men wear generally a *nguo* only, that is a loin cloth of white or blue calico. Women wear a *kisuto*, or long cloth of blue, or printed, or coloured calico wrapped tightly round the body, immediately under the arms, and on the head an *ukaya*, a piece of blue calico with two long ends. It has a string passing under the chin, to which a silver ornament, *jebu*, is attached.[30]

Nguo mbili were later called *kisutu* as Steere's vocabulary list on cloth and clothing in Zanzibar shows: *Kisuto* or *kisutu*, plural *visutu*, a large piece of printed calico, often forming a woman's whole dress. It is printed and colored. He also translates five other items of Zanzibar costume:

> *Doti,* a loin cloth, a piece of cloth a little less than two yards long[31] *Kaniki,* a dark blue calico cloth *Kanzu,* a dress for a man or woman *Leso,* a handkerchief as in *leso ya kufutia kamasi,* a pocket handkerchief (Literally: cloth for wiping the nose)[32] *Nguo,* calico, cotton cloth, clothes as in *nguo ya meza,* a tablecloth, *nguo ya maki,* stout cloth, *kutenda nguo* to stretch the [cotton] threads for weaving.

Both Krapf and Steere give *nguo* for clothes but Steere also includes two further terms *kisutu* and *doti*. The first is related to the Arabic *kiswatun* in its form and meaning and the second has been identified as Hindi by Johnson and Persian.[33] In Swahili, *kiswatun* has two derivations *kisutu* and *kiswa*. At this time, the word *leso* meant a handkerchief.

Steere provides a third name for *nguo mbili,* a garment of "two pieces". This is *kisutu*, which might have preceded *leso* and *kanga* chronologically to mean a garment worn by women. *Kisutu* appeared in both the 1869 and 1881 dictionaries. It also appeared in a Swahili song, *"Utumbuizo wa Gungu"* included among Steere's *Swahili Tales from Zanzibar.*[34]

Akiinuwa mkonowe mwana   Kaupeka juu la mwanzi.
 Akaangua **kisuto** cha Kaye,   Cha kinisi chema matorazi,
Ka'mweka kituzo cha mato,   Buni ami, mwana wa shangazi.
Ki mwambia, bwana na tukae   Siimemno, ukataajazi.

Steere gives the following translation:

And the mistress lifts up her hand,   She puts it up to the bamboo,
She takes down a large cloth (**kisutu**)   of ancient work with a beautiful border
                                        woven around it.
And he puts a handkerchief to her eye, the child of his father and child of his
                                        aunt.[35]
And she says to him, "Master, let us sit down   Do not stand over much, and make
                                        yourself tired.[36]

The reader may recall that Steere describes *kisuto* as a large piece of calico about two yards square, wrapped tightly round the body immediately below the armpits, and reaching the ankles. It may be of blue or of printed calico and has a beautiful border. This confirms Burton's observation that *kisutu* is a form of women's dress he sees in Zanzibar in 1856. He writes about it at length:

> The Murungawanah, [*muungwana*] or free born [women]…is distinguished out-of-doors by her rude mantilla, and 'ladies' affect an *Ukaya*, or fillet of indigo-dyed cotton, or muslin, somewhat like that of the Somal and the Syrians. The feminine garb is a **Kisutu,** or length of stained cotton, blue and red being the pet colours. It resembles the *kitambi* of Malagash, and it is the nearest approach to the primitive African kilt of skin or tree bark. Wrapped tightly round the unsupported bosom and extending from the armpits to the heels, this ungraceful garb depresses the breast, spoils the figure, and conceals nothing of the deficiencies.[37]

This, of course, is only Burton's personal opinion!

Let us now return to our dictionaries to examine entries that provide not only content but also with the context of time and place. By 1881, Krapf's list of Zanzibar costume had expanded to include:

> *kisua*, a suit of clothes
> **kisutu** or **kisuto**: a kind of coloured cloth, a large piece of printed calico
> **lesso** (properly *laesso*): a handkerchief
> **nguo**: cloth, especially cotton cloth or clothes

Krapf's list introduces us to sophisticated urban styles of dress. Including *kisutu* he names nineteen other kinds of cloth: *kisu'tu, kiswa, lungi, she'doro, kikoi, debua'ni, bersa'ti, kitambi cha iwishoa, mpunga, tausiri masna'fi, sebaaia ya mtande wa kilili, Ka'nike, Isma'eli, usso wa nianni, sa'hare, shuke za mfundo or mandundu, bafuda dondo, Amerikano, Lamali and shotara*. Most of these he adds, are exported from India and Arabia. He defines *kisua* as a suit of clothes and *kisutu* or *kisuto* as a kind of coloured cloth, a large piece of printed calico.[38]

At this point we leave consideration of indigenous Swahili garment terms to see what other garments from other cultures have been introduced. A vast new costume vocabulary is added to the local repertoire.

Krapf does not include *kanga* as cloth in his rich list of textiles. Elsewhere, he has three entries for the word:

1. *kanga la mnazi*: the switch-like end of a cocoa-branch (sic) from which the *vidako* shoot forth and from which the cocoa-liquor is obtained.
2. *kanga*: guinea-fowl; *niuni wa vitone tone* (a bird with dots)
3. *kanga:* (verb) to fry, roast, to burn by roasting.

Nor does Krapf include *leso* in his list of garment textiles. *He* spells *leso* as *lesso* or *laesso* and identifies it as a handkerchief: lesso *ya kufuta makamasi* (a cloth for wiping nose) a pocket-hand-kerchief and he uses four terms—*nguo, doti, shuka,* and *kisutu* for a wrap round cloth worn by both men and women.

This leads us to infer that the term *kanga* for cloth has not yet been introduced in 1882. Can we unearth when that innovation occurred?

The movement of people across the Indian Ocean for the purposes of trade and settlement led to the spread both of goods and of the languages that identified them. Thus, any similarity that exists between the Arabic and Swahili-speaking peoples around its coasts is to be seen not only in the vocabulary of their two languages but in their concepts and usage as a result of their rich culture contact.

Writing in 1873, Charles New, the author of *Life Wandering & Labours in Eastern Africa,* makes it clear that the Waswahili adopted the dress style of the Arabs, a process first mentioned by Owen in 1822. Living in close proximity as they did along the East African coast, this was a case of African residents emulating the dress of their upper class Muslim visitors. He provides a detailed description of the costume:

> In dress, the Wasuahili copy the Arabs. We will first describe that of the men. First, a loincloth, with coloured border, called **kikoi,** is drawn round the waist, and fastened by folding both ends together, rolling them into a ball at the top, and tucking it inwards against the body. Next over this is drawn the **kansu** [*kanzu*], a long, straight, narrow garment, of various materials, but often of white calico, with short tight sleeves, looking not unlike what is worn among ourselves for a nightdress. Upon this is worn a **kisbao** [*kizibau*], a kind of sleeveless waistcoat, of bright colours, elaborate braiding, and showy buttons. Sometimes this gives place to a sleeved jacket of crimson or purple broadcloth. A shawl is often twisted round the waist in the form of a girdle. On great occasions, and generally on Friday, which is the Muhammadan [Muslim] Sabbath, the **joho** is worn. This is a long overcoat of fine cloth, may be of blue, black, scarlet, or purple, sometimes richly ornamented over the shoulders with gold lace, open in front, but falling over the back in one seamless piece, and reaching to the very heels. On the poll of their heads, they wear sometimes **a red fez**, and sometimes a white needle worked cap, called **kofia,** and about this is bound the **kilemba** or turban, a large cloth of white, but more often of highly coloured material. On their feet, they wear large, thick, cumbrous sandals, the borders, straps, and tongues of which are rather tastefully ornamented with interlacing of coloured leather. Such is the Msuahili of the male gender when completely dressed. In his

perambulations about town, he carries either his **upanga** (sword) or a **bakora** (walking stick) He deems himself a superb grandee.[39]

This is a very thorough account of an elegantly dressed Mswahili man. Both the language and the colors convey a cosmopolitan, a man of the world. But then the author adds:

> Of course, there are many modifications of this dress and get-up. The **kansu** and skullcap are all that is worn indoors, and often all that is worn out of doors. The loincloth (presumably, *shuka)* has not to do service alone, even among respectable people; while, with regard to the slave, it is all that he can procure. Some slaves, however, do better, and now and then they make as grand an appearance as their masters.[40]

Charles New also describes two styles in Swahili women's dress that he discerned in 1873: that of the upper class and that of the majority:

> The better class of [Waswahili] women wears *suruali* (trousers), and *kansu(kanzu)* of coloured material. Upon their heads, they bind, so as to hide their hair, silk handkerchiefs, or wear caps spangled with gold. Tunics, tastefully embroidered, are also worn, and Muhammadan (sic) delicacy requires that this class should be masked. Sandals of leather, but sometimes wood, or clogs, adorn the feet. Out of doors, a large square black silk mantle is thrown over all, but women of this grade are seldom seen abroad. The majority of the women dress in inferior style to this. *Visuto* (plural of *kisutu)*, square coloured cloths, and *kaniki*, indigo-dyed stuffs, are common articles of dress; but *lesu,* large coloured cotton handkerchiefs, are much affected. Six of the latter cut into two parts of three each, are sewn together so as to make one square cloth and the dress is complete. This is drawn round the body under the arms, and is secured by gathering the ends together and rolling them into a ball at the chest. A similar article is worn over the shoulders, or is hung from the head like a veil. In some places, the **ukaya** is preferred. This is, generally speaking, a long piece of blue calico or gauze, fastened over the forehead by a piece of cord round the chin, and falling over the head down the back. Dressed in this style, particularly when the material is new and the colours are bright, the Msuahili woman is in her glory, and appears to admire herself prodigiously.[41]

Two special points are of interest here. First, the author does not mention *kanga* in his account of women's clothes. He, however, does mention **visutu,** the plural of **kisutu**. He describes it as a square colored cloth. He also mentions **lesu** as consisting of three large colored cotton handkerchiefs. Note that New describes the cloth as square; but today's *kanga* is rectangular in shape. Moreover, three pieces joined together do not make a square. Nevertheless, his description of how the *kisutu* is worn closely resembles Burton's description of it in 1856 and Steere's in 1869. **Kisuto** or **kisutu** signified a large piece of printed colored cloth that had a beautiful border and was used to cover the body and the head. It could have been blue, red, plain or decorated. Steere, it will be recalled, identified **kisutu** as a garment and **lesu** as a handkerchief.

Second, the word **kisutu** that both Burton and Steere use later came to refer specifically to a particular *kanga* design. Here we have two labels for the same or similar item of clothing but one acquiring a new meaning. Printed in three colors, red, black and white, this usually had seventeen rows of small crosses.(See Figure 1). The late Fatma Shaaban Abdullah, an artist from Zanzibar, believed that the small crosses commemorated a time when Zanzibar was struck by plague and victims were carried to quarantine in Red Cross vans.[42] This would most likely have been during the cholera epidemic that struck Zanzibar in 1869.

It appears the Swahili language had three alternative terms for the "two cloth garment" *nguo* **mbili**. These were **kisutu, doti** and **leso/lesu**. There was also an extremely rich vocabulary for different kinds of fabric. But again, there is no mention of **kanga** as two pieces of cloth that are sold as one and have to be cut with scissors in order to make a pair to wear. The term *kanga,* so well known today, must have appeared later. **Kisutu** chronologically preceded **leso** and **kanga** in use as a garment.

In order to establish further the chronology and semantic connection of **kisutu** with **leso** and **kanga** in East Africa we turn to Swahili literature to find that at the end of the nineteenth century the words **leso** and **kanga** appear together in a poem by an anonymous Swahili poet (circa 1890).[43] Two verses relevant to this discussion read as follows:

Verse 4*:*   *Jahazi chombo kikuu hakihimili kubisha.*
Lataka tanga la kati na pepo za kuelekeza
Pepo zake nyiminyimi kama unga wa kusaga.
*Bibi wanifunga **leso**, mkufu waniumiza*

Verse 5:   *Nilipokwenda njiani nilisikia parakacha:*
*Hageuka hatazama haona **kanga** akata.*
Kanipendeza wajihi na maungo kutakata.
Kope na macho na mboni zilikuwaje kuteta?

These may be translated as follows:

Verse 4:   The dhow is a big vessel; that cannot stand a hard push.
It requires a middle sail and winds to propel it.
The winds it needs are as soft as ground flour.
Lady, you are tying a **leso** (round me); the chain hurts me.

Verse 5:   When I walked along the road, I heard a rustling sound.
I turned and looked. I saw a **kanga** crossing.
She had a pleasing face and well formed body.
Eyelashes, eyes and pupils why are they not in harmony?

In this poem *leso* in verse 4 refers to a cloth but we do not know whether it is the size of a handkerchief (as described by Krapf and Steere) or larger. *Kanga* in verse 5 is a beautiful example of synecdoche in Swahili. The part (the clothing) is taken for the whole (the woman). A Swahili riddle from Zanzibar says:

Nimekwenda njiani, nimeona kisuto; mwenyi kisuto sikumwona.
As I went on my way, I saw *kisuto*; the wearer of the cloth (*kisuto*) I did not see.[44]

We now move into the twentieth century in our pursuit of the elusive *kanga*. In 1907, Ethel Younghusband accompanied her husband to East Africa. He was then serving in the King's African Rifles and they lived first on the Kenya coast and then in Zanzibar. She has the following to say about women's dress in her book *Glimpses of East Africa and Zanzibar* (1908).

> The women in East Africa simply wear two cloths or **"kangas,"** one tied under both arms, and the other thrown over their necks and arms. But in Zanzibar they copy the Arab dress more closely, and often **have one** *kanga* **made into a little tight dress to their knees, the other flung artistically over their shoulders,** and almost skin-tight trousers with large frills round the ankles, ornamented with embroidery; round their heads they wear a twisted oblong of brightly coloured cloth, set at an angle, and odd cords and tassels, a most picturesque dress, as they are most particular about the colours and patterns.

This is one of the clearest descriptions of how a *kanga* was worn. Note also how appreciative the description of the costume is. Historically, this is the first womans-eye description we have of **a pair of** *kanga*. It is also the first explicit statement of the use of the term *kanga* to refer to two pieces of cloth worn as a garment in East Africa. We may assume, then, that the term *kanga* was known in both Kenya and Zanzibar and that *nguo mbili*—the two cloths recalled from the past only in a children's song—have by the end of the nineteenth century acquired the generic name of *kanga.*

Like *kisutu*, and *leso* the word *kanga* is derived from Arabic. The term *kharqah* or *khalqah* in Omani Arabic means 'piece of cloth'. It is derived from *kharq* 'to tear or to split' It was also, as we have seen (Introduction) a Fulani word for a type of cloth in West Africa, *kherka*. When introduced into the Swahili language, to refer to the two pieces of cloth that were earlier known in Swahili as *nguo mbili,* the word changed phonologically:

kharqah>khalqah>khalqa>khanqa >khanga>kanga.

Its old spelling as *khanga* still appears in the written form on some *kangas*. Subsequently, *kanga* came to mean specifically two cloths with borders joined together as one piece that we know today.

In short, the item of clothing that Swahili speakers today identify as *kanga* was first known simply as *nguo mbili,* then as *kisutu, doti* and *leso,* and only later as *kanga*. To this day the term *leso* is used synonymously with *kanga* in both Mombasa and Oman but not in Zanzibar.

Yet are *kanga* and *leso* identical? Our attention has already been drawn to the marketing of *kangas*. In 1907 Carl Velten in his book, *Prosa und Poesie der Suaheli* stated that one *korja* (twenty items) of *kanga* sold for eight *reales*[45] while twenty items of *leso* sold for five. If these had been identical types of clothing, they would not have differed in price.[46] The readers recall well both Krapf and Steere identified *leso* as a handkerchief and we may assume that this was an apt translation in the nineteenth century when Velten included the word in his list of trade goods. When, then, did *leso* become a regional alternative to *kanga*?

As we see from the literary documents, all five terms *nguo mbili, kisutu, doti, leso* and *kanga* meant originally generically cloth and clothing and only later came to specify different types of cloths or garments. The term *kisutu*, for example, first referred simply to a cloth with a beautiful border. It was only later applied to a specific design that appeared on a *kanga* worn by a bride on her wedding day.

Captain J. E. E. Craster writing in 1913 on his first day in Pemba (an island lying to the north of Zanzibar) observed that:

> The women were dressed in cotton cloths wrapped round them close under their arms and reaching to the knees. The patterns on these cloths were very large and brightly coloured. Some of them were merely huge circles of colour, or simple geometrical patterns, but the more elaborate were representations of some adjunct of civilization. One of the most popular was a picture of an electric light standard, with a large arc light in a wired globe hanging from it.[47]

What is of interest here is the evolution of the patterned *kanga* carrying the design of an electric bulb clearly indicating an innovation of the time. We are beginning to see on the cloth indications of 20th century technology. The garment presents a permanent record of a current event. If we are to understand the evolution of *kanga* nomenclature of East Africa through its linguistic expression it is necessary to know the changing language of commerce particularly descriptions of cloth as merchandise. Craster's description fits *nguo mbili,* 'the two garments', but he does not identify them by name as *kangas* or *lesos.*

Notes

1. This corrects Rose Marie Beck's suggestion that *leso* appeared in Zanzibar around 1875. See her " Aesthetics of Communication: Text and Textiles (Leso) from the East African Coast (Swahili)", *Research in African Literatures* 31.3 (Winter 2000) 104-124. I also refer the reader to Julia Hilgar's comments in the Introduction note 11 that *kanga* emerged in the 1850s.
2. Johnson, *A Standard Swahili-English* Dictionary (London, 1939) translates *ambika* as 'brought into contact, hold together, be stuck together.'
3. I discuss the work of Al-Idris and Ibn BaTTuTa in my manuscript *Kiswahili Contact and Change.*
4. B.H. Robinson, (ed.), Owen, W.F.W., *Narratives of Voyages to Explore the Shores of Africa, Arabia and Madagascar* (New York, 1833).
5. The Oxford Dictionary states that almug is an error and should be algum which it defines as a tree mentioned in Bible (2 Chron.ii 8; 1 Kings x.) It describes the tree as a kind of sandalwood and it derives the word *algum* from the Sanskrit *valguka.* It is more likely that the word *almug* is the correct form and derives from *al-muql,* a gum tree. Gum Arabic was an important item of the Indian Ocean trade.
6. Duarte Barbosa, *The Coasts of East Africa and Malabar* (London, 1866) 4.
7. Ibid. 6.
8. Ibid. 11.
9. Ibid. 14.
10. This letter was among several I received from Edward A. Alpers during my research in 1976.
11. In this transcript gh, f, and b represent today's Standard Swahili sounds g,v, and p, which do not appear in Arabic script.
12. Ibid.
13. Owen, *Narrative of Voyages* (New York,1833) 10.
15 Ibid. 171.
14. Ibid. 171.
15. Burton, *Zanzibar, City, Island and Coast* (London, 1872) 414.
16. Burton, *The Lake Region of Central Africa: A Picture of Exploration* (London, 1860).
17. Salem, Massachusetts was an important nineteenth century port. Sailors and traders from there exercised major commercial role in African and Arabian markets.

18. Ibid. 148.

19. Ibid. 148-149.

20. Ibid.

21. Ibid. 149.

22. Burton, *The Lake Regions* Vol. I (London 1872) 150.

23. Johnson derives the word *jora* from Hindi *juwr,* "a length of calico in the piece of about 30 yards."

24. The change of Arabic sound /uw/ to /o/ in Swahili is a phonological change seen in other cognates such as *suwq> soko* "market", *Tuhuwr> tohara* "cleanness" *huwdaar> hodari* "clever" *huwd>hodi* "safely" and *shuwq> shoka* "an axe". In this example, *jurra* becomes *jora* or *gora*.

25. Burton, *The Lake Regions,* Vol. II (London, 1872) 310-311.

26. Sharifa Zawawi, *African Muslim Names* (Trenton, *1991*) x*ii, xiv.*

27. L.J. Krapf, *Six East African Languages* (London, 1850).

28. Edward Steere, *Swahili Tales* (London, 1869).

29. Krapf, 1881, identified *doti* as a piece of cotton-cloth eight *mikono* (cubits) or a little less than four yards in length. 52.

30. This entry in Steere's dictionary invalidates Rose-Marie Beck's claim (n.1 above) that *leso* appeared in Zanzibar around 1875.

31. Bernard Krumm, *Words of Oriental Origin in Swahil* (London, 1940).

32. Steere, *Swahili Tales* (London, 1869).

33. The phrase *buni ami*, means cousin, father's brother's and mother's sister's son. This implies a marriage of cousins.

34. Steere, *Swahili Tale* (London, 1869) p.499.

35. See Burton, *Zanzibar* Vol. I (London, 1872) 434.

36. L. Krapf, *Suahili Language* (London, 1882) 158.

37. See Charles New, *Life Wandering & Labours in Eastern Africa* (London, 873) pp.57-58.

38. Charles New, *Life Wandering* (London, 1873) 58-59.

39. Ibid. 60.

40. Fatma Shaaban Abdullah, "Reflections on a symbol," *Africa Now,* February *1984,* 50.

41. Carl G. Buttner, *Umschrift undUebersetzung der arabisch geschriebenen, Suaheli Schriftstuc,* (Berlin, *1892*).

42. This may be found in Steere.

43. A Real, a form of currency, was a silver coin used in East Africa around the nineteenth century.

44. Carl Velten, *Prosa und Poesie der Suaheli* (Swahili Prose and Poetry) (Berlin, 1907) These two items *kanga* and *leso* appear among a large collection of different types of cloths with their prices on 221.

45. J.E.E. Craster, *Pemba. The Spice Island of Zanzibar* (London, 1913) 40.

46. Ibid. Carl Velten. These two items *kanga* and *leso* appear among a large collection of different types of cloths with their prices on 221.

47. J.E.E. Craster, *Pemba. The Spice Island of Zanzibar* (London, 1913) 40.

CHAPTER THREE

KANGA MOTIFS, NAMES AND FASHIONS

In the first section of this chapter I describe the *kanga* motifs. In the second, I discuss their *majina,* "names" and in the third I examine fashion, the taste of the wearer. *Kangas* are traditionally and most commonly made out of a cotton fabric of two rectangular lengths joined together as a pair. In size a pair of *kangas* is sixty to sixty five inches long and forty two to forty five inches in width. The original Swahili term for their mode of production was *nguo mbili.* To separate the two pieces the buyer or receiver of *kanga* cuts at the dotted line. Each piece is long enough to wrap around the body or to wear as a shawl. *Kangas* for Oman are often made of a thin cotton fabric because of the long hot summers there.

Kanga Designs and Colors

Kangas are never plain but always display a geometrical or floral design that is repeated in the same colors on both sides of the pair. The most common designs are of fruit, flowers, and everyday objects or they are abstract geometrical designs similar to those used on local mats, baskets and doors. These are symmetrical and simple. Fatma Shaaban Abdullah suggests that "A *kanga* textile design is different from other textile printed fabrics in that it portrays a characteristic of African design: divisions and panels; repetitions of motifs and use of stripes to separate the sequence of panels."[1]

A *kanga* gets its first 'name' (*jina*) — its generic name — from its foreground, the object represented in the design. This is known as *mji* (the city or town). Whatever the design on a *kanga*, its four borders (*ma-pindo* i.e. the hems) are all of the same design and color as the foreground. The *mji* may have a centerpiece. This may be fruit. For example:

embe	mango
chenza	tangerine
fenesi	jack fruit
kungu	Indian almond
muhindi	corn/maize
korosho	cashew nut
njugu	peanuts
mbaazi	pigeon peas
pilipili	hot pepper

or flowers. For example

yungi yungi	water lily
wardi	rose
asumini	jasmine
kilua	kilua

or household objects. For example:

msala	prayer mat
zulia	carpet
mtungi	water pitcher
vibakuli	small bowls
sahani	plates
sinia	tray
msumeno	saw

At one time *kanga* designs were printed in only three or four colors-usually red , green, yellow or black. Today, the number and range of designs and colors has greatly increased and *kangas* are radiant in mauve, turquoise, brown, blue, beige, fuchsia, maroon, olive and orange. One *kanga* I received as a gift from Oman has a design in reddish brown, light brown, beige, olive green and black. Five colors in all. It has a beautiful blush of brilliant and bright colors that brighten a dull moment. Another *kanga* shows roses, some dark and some light red, set against dark and light turquoise among turquoise leaves. The foreground is a geometrical design in beige. Its borders are of red roses with turquoise leaves. Counting the light hues as separate shades, this *kanga* has six colors.

The color scheme on *kangas* is not necessarily true to the objects shown except in the case of flags where colors themselves convey symbolic meaning. On the flag of Tanzania, black represents the people, green represents land, yellow represents the economy and wealth, and blue represents the ocean that unites the Tanganyika mainland with Zanzibar and Pemba. On Kenya's flag black represents the people, yellow represents wealth, red represents the blood of those who died during the Mau Mau wars of independence, and white represents unity and peace.[2] Oman's flag its colors are red, green, and white. The red was the color of the old Omani flag and symbolizes the nation's battles in its long history.[3] The color green symbolizes green land and prosperity and the white symbolizes peace and happiness. Colors on *kangas* are of no symbolic significance.

Kanga Majina Names

If a *kanga* gets its first generic name from its design, it acquires its second name from the written message it bears. In Swahili this is called *jina*. This name was always printed within a rectangular frame just above the cloth's lower border. Traditionally *kangas* carried a message or saying written in Arabic script. This provided its second Swahili *'jina'*. (See Appendix A). Today few *kangas* appear without a message. A typical old *kanga* is shown in Figure 3. It has three colors red, black and white. Its 'name' is written in Arabic script and so runs from right to left. It may be transcribed in Swahili as :

Kukopa furaha kulipa matanga
Borrowing is a joy but paying back is grief

The *kanga* in Figure 4 is called *Msumeno,* a saw, because its foreground design resembles the teeth of a saw. It says:

Wema hauozi
Goodness does not go bad

Here it is in green, yellow and black but it is also made in other colors, with different border designs and *jina*. Another version of this design in different colors and with a different border says:

Neno limesemwa ndani limefikaje hadharani
The word was spoken indoors, how did it reach the public?

Yet a third version of *msumeno* (a saw) says:
Dunia ni maarifa
The world is an experience

Because of a ritual restriction on praying in clothes that depict living images, it is rare to find human portraits or animal figures on *kangas*. An exception occurs with commemorative *kanga* designs. These may represent living images. A *kanga* from Tanzania commemorating the death of Mwalimu Julius Kambarage Nyerere, the first president of Tanzania was printed in 1999. His portrait provides the centerpiece of the design with the flag of Tanzania on either side of it (Figure 5). Figure 6 provides another exceptional example. A commemorative *kanga* of the late 1950s. It shows a red rooster, the emblem of the Zanzibar Nationalist Party.

There were three political parties in Zanzibar at that time: the Zanzibar Nationalist Party (ZNP), the Zanzibar and Pemba Peoples' Party (ZPPP) and the Afro-Shirazi Party (ASP). After the 1961 elections the Z.N.P. and Z.P.P.P. coalesced, to become Z.N.P./Z.P.P. P. alliance. The opposition party (ASP) had a *kanga* as well. Its symbol was a well *kisima*. In the early 1960s, a *kanga* produced in Dar es Salaam celebrated Tanganyika's independence from colonial rule. It showed a freedom torch and a flag. The message on it read:

Umoja wa Tanu una nguvu kama mzinga
Tanu's unity is as strong as a gun

In her article "Reflection on a Symbol", Fatma Shaaban Abdullah observes, "Most of the motifs [on *kangas*] are symbolic, *especially along the borders*." She herself produced a *kanga* design for Tanzania depicting a large freedom torch as a centerpiece with small freedom torches repeated along the borders. A burst of arrowheads surrounded the centerpiece filling the rest of the foreground. She interprets both its design and the message:

Twalipenda Azimio la Arusha
We like the Arusha Declaration

Commemorative *kangas* such as those shown above and that in Figure 7 are reminders of past events. They provide historical references. Both the wearer and those who see the design and read the text relive vivid memories of what might otherwise have been long forgotten. History is propagated anew.

Before the 1960s the *jina* name appeared in Swahili written in Arabic script as we saw in Figure 3.[4] The shift from Arabic to Roman letters did not occur until late in the 1950s in both Kenya and Tanzania. This was when European education became predominant in East Africa and a larger number of girls began attending Western schools. Before this time, the written medium of communication was largely Swahili in Arabic script. Western education brought in the use of Roman script in government offices. Arabic script continued to be used to reach the families in the fields who could not read the western script but were literate in Swahili-Arabic script. Paradoxically, most of the *kangas* produced in India for Omani traders bear Roman not Arabic script. This may be a continuation of a long established tradition innovated in East Africa and carried later to the Gulf States. Only a few *kangas* produced in Muscat or Salala bear *'jina'* written in Arabic.

Mahfoudha H. Alley, a Zanzibari poetess and politician, writes in her article on "The Power of Kanga" that the man responsible for introducing such *kanga* messages was the late Abdullah Kaderina (Abdulkader).[5] She identifies Kaderina as the pioneer owner of a *kanga* shop at Biashara Street in Mombasa in 1887. Laura Fair, a historian gives a different date. "…sometime in the1910s." she writes.[6]

Kangas with *jina* names are known in Swahili as *kanga zenye maandishi* (*kangas* with writing). The names express in a poetic style a situation, theme or concept. The composition has frequently a parallel structure:

Hasira hasara
Anger is regret

Dunia ni Maarifa
The world is an experience

Wema hauozi
Goodness does not go bad

Akili ni mali
Intelligence is wealth

Many of the *majina* names are ancient proverbs. For example,

Mpiga ngumi ukuta huumiza mkonowe
He who strikes a wall hurts his own hand

Mtafunwa na nyoka akiona ung'ongo hustuka
He who is bitten by a snake is scared of a straw
[Once beaten twice shy]

Aliye juu mngojee chini
He who is high up, you wait for him below

Debe shinda haliachi kutika
An empty cask makes most noise

Even today in Oman and the Comoro Islands, the *jina* name is sometimes written in Arabic script on some *kangas*. A *kanga* from Comoro bearing Arabic script is shown in Figure 8.

Salama salimina
Safe and sound

This is a message sent to a friend or relative who has returned safely from a journey. A wife may wear it on her husband's return from abroad.

A similar message is shown on a *kanga* from Oman on which the language is Arabic but the *jina* is written in Roman script (Figure 9). It says:

Alhamdulillah 'ala ssalaama
Thank God, you are safe

This is said on meeting a traveler who has just arrived, a woman who has had a baby, or someone who is safe after an accident or trauma.

Another *kanga* from Oman conveys local hospitality (Figure 10.) It shows an Omani coffee pot. The message is in Arabic language and script. It says:

Delle 'Umaaniyya ba'da l'uwd maa fiy qu'uwd
Omani coffee pot, do not prolong your stay
after you have been served coffee and
brought the sweet smelling incense

This reflects a traditional Omani and Islamic custom that visitors should not overstay their welcome after the coffee and *'uwd l-bukhuwr* the sweet smelling incense wood that always follows a meal.

Although in selecting their *kangas*, women buying them are more attracted to the colors than the design, they are also concerned over choosing the right *jina* with the right message.
What are these 'names'? Who formulates them and prints them? Who uses them and to whom do they apply?

The tradition of inscribing clothes has existed throughout several civilizations and, in the Islamic world, for centuries. Inscriptions were first used to glorify kings and sultans, and to pray that the person honored by the cloth might have long life, strength, health, prosperity, success, happiness and joy. Such inscriptions appear not only on clothes but also on coins, utensils, rugs, carpets, tapestries, banners and prayer mats. They were used on leather, porcelain, pottery, metal and wood. Inscriptions adorned the outside of buildings as well as ceilings and thresholds. Some doors carried inscriptions to ward off unwelcome guests with evil intentions.

One may say that, with *kangas*, the Waswahili have maintained this custom of inscribing cloth but have democratized it since *kangas* are the everyday apparel of ordinary people - and particularly women. The texts that appear on *kangas* are sent to the textile factory by local traders. The name of the trader who commissioned a *kanga* may appear in one of its corners along with the place where it was manufactured and a number that identifies the design.

At one time *kanga* designs and *jina* names were collected from local artists and from High School students who were paid a small fee to produce them. I remember practising my art work and earning a little bit of pocket money for my *kanga* designs and *majina* when I was in High School in Zanzibar. The messages actually printed reflect the agents' final selections from those that they have received and thus represent their own views of what will sell rather than the views of the designers and those who had passed them on to them.

Nevertheless, one assumes that since these *kangas* are meant to attract women customers [or buyers] and are for mass consumption, the manufacturers select names that represent the likely feelings and views of the average women.

These inscriptions on clothes confirm and strengthen established relationships. They describe and reflect specific features of social relations and, as a result, establish elements of behavioral expectation in systems of strict and multifaceted social interaction. Thus, for example, the *kanga* that declares:

Ukipata cheo usisahau mkeo
Do not forget your wife when you get your promotion

They epitomize the vitality of Swahili composition and expression and are thus an integral part of Swahili traditional and contemporary literature.

Kanga Fashions and Good Taste

Although it is important to emphasize at this point that the messages *kangas* convey are not exclusively those of women, as some authors claim, fashionably and tastefully dressed women like to match their *kangas* with the rest of their outfits. For them, the relation of the design to the color is not a determining factor, in whether or not they buy a certain *kanga*. This is not new. As earlier as 1905, a European in government service in Zanzibar, Robert Nunez Lyne, noted in his book *Zanzibar in Contemporary Times* that:

> Women are simply clad in two square cloths of colored calico, one of which is tucked under the arms, and the other thrown over the shoulders. They are very particular about the patterns of the prints, the fashions of which change every few months. The fashions of the men's clothes never change, but the women, as in other countries, are the slaves of fashion; and I have no doubt Zanzibar sets the fashion for all that part of the world, as Paris does for Europe. The people of Zanzibar are in more prosperous circumstances than those on the mainland, and dress better.[7]

Indeed even today *kangas* change faster than any other fashions. Yet the layout of the four borders is always retained, consistency prevails and tradition is maintained.

Ethel Younghusband writing of Mombasa in 1908 reports that the manager of an English firm that exported *kangas* told her that:

> The ladies are so fastidious, they will not wear the kangas when the fashion has passed, several thousands of one pattern are ordered the first time, but it never pays to re-order. Patterns of flowers or dogs do not sell; generally, their taste is good, but just now it is rather startling, brilliant reds and yellow mixed with black happen to be the latest style. Sometimes large patterns of trains, or ships appear just spread over the broadest part of their bodies.[8]

In one respect, at least, not much has changed since the English manufacturer made his observations. New, fashionable – and more costly *kanga*—are still preferred for social functions and for gifts. No woman will wear the same *kanga* twice to public functions.

Today, every month sees new *kangas,* new designs and new '*jina*'. I remember when I was a child in Zanzibar witnessing momentous happenings that accompanied the appearance of every new *kanga* on the market. It was a song and dance act. It was an occasion. A salesman, Hamadi Makongoro, carried the latest *kanga* from house to house throughout Zanzibar Town announcing its arrival. Singing out the name of the *kanga,* he described the new design: *Msumeno,* a saw, *Korosho,* cashew nut, *Bakuli,* a bowl – straight off the *meli,* (the steamer). The arrival of each ship from overseas brought new *kangas.*

Nowadays, alas, because of the abundance of *kangas,* there is no door-to-door announcement, no singing and dancing at each new *kanga's* arrival. Instead, they are displayed on shop counters, hung from the windows and doors of fabric stores, and from poles jutting out into the street. Figure 11 shows a number of *kangas* on sale at one time in Darajani's street in Zanzibar. Note the range of colors.

Although a woman is primarily trying to project a message to those with whom she is most in contact whether women friends, neighbors, relatives, children, husband or boy friend, when she goes into a store to buy a pair of *kanga* or several pairs of *kangas* she is attracted first by color and design. The message only comes later to reinforce her choice. When she knows what the *kanga* says she may also ask for it by the message not by the name of the design. If the message does not please her, she casts aside the *kanga.* She does not want to buy unpopular messages.

I counted and recorded the names of some of the *kangas* of just one of my friends in Oman in order to explore her taste. I looked at fifty-five pairs: eight were *kanga bubu* [i.e. without messages.] My friend, Mukhlisa, told me that she received most of her *kangas* as gifts from relatives and friends. She also bought *kangas* to give away as gifts, and the only time she purchased a pair of *kangas* for herself was when she came across a name that expressed her own feelings at that moment. One of her favorites said:

Masikini wa bahati tajiri wa matatizo
(I am) poor in luck and rich in problems

When she was younger Mukhlisa used to go by colors and designs in her selection, but now she pays more attention to the name. This is because of an incident that occurred to her a couple of years ago. She had asked someone to buy her a pair of *kangas* and to deliver them, on her behalf, to her sister-in-law, in Zanzibar. The sister-in-law was upset by when she received the gift. The *kangas* bore the *jina*:

Hasidi kwangu hupati kitu
Envious person, you will not get anything from me

Her sister-in-law complained to Mukhlisa's mother-in-law, who later passed on the message to Mukhlisa. From that day to this, my friend does not give a *kanga* as a gift without checking what it says. She is now careful always to choose *kanga* gifts herself, by its message not by its colors or design.

Sometimes it is necessary for a mother, an aunt or a bride's godmother to select an appropriate *kanga* design and message for a special occasion. One mother I know recently commissioned a *kanga* to be worn by her women guests at her daughter's marriage. (See Figure 12). It read:

Tumeamua tuishi wawili tusiwafuate wachochezi
We have decided to live together as two people and not to follow those
who incite trouble

The *kanga* was worn on one of the three days' wedding celebration. On that day, we, the friends and relatives, wore this *kanga* over our dresses in the morning when the betrothal ceremony was taking place. This practice of wearing a *sare* chosen by a relative of the bride or groom's is a common practice at weddings among the Waswahili.[9] It reflects the guests' solidarity and support for the bride as well as the bride's mother's affection towards them. At this particular wedding the mother provided the friends with free *kangas* to wear but usually *kangas* for *sare* are commissioned through a store so that relatives and friends may purchase them for themselves. The chosen *kanga* is an important social symbol at a wedding.

> *Harusi ni nguo ya kheri*
> A wedding is a blessed garment

This was demonstrated by East African women in a modern blended cultural event that took place recently in the United States. The sister of the bride organizing the wedding shower held a *kanga* party. Although some of the guests brought gifts in the American fashion, the bride's East African friends came dressed in *kangas*. She herself had a sufficient supply of *kangas* at home to provide her American guests with them to wear on the happy occasion. (See Figure 13 of A Boston Shower Party). Wherever they are in the world, *kangas* allow Waswahili to nourish and maintain literary and folkloric traditions.

Notes

1. Fatma Sahaaban Abdullah, "Reflections on a Symbol," *Africa Now, February* (1984) 49.
2. See Sharifa Zawawi, *Jifunze Kiswahili Chetu* (Trenton, 1990) 80.
3. See http://www.omannews.com/arabic/oman%20flagA.htm. This new flag was raised for the first time on A.D. December 17, 1970 (A.H. 18 shawwal, 1319).
4. This is a much later date than that in the 1930's suggested by Hilgar.
5. Hon. Mahfoudha H Alley,"The Power of `Kanga', in *The City*, (Mombasa, n.d.)13.
6. Laura Fair, *Past Times* (Ohio, 2001) 80.
7. Robert Nunez Lyne, Zanzibar in Contemporary Times, 234.
8. Ethel Younghusband, *Glimpse* (London,1908) 35. There are many *kanga* designs of flowers these days but not of animals and especially dogs whom the Muslims regard as unclean.
9. The term *sare* is used to refer to ' same' and in this case the women wore the same *kanga* design. Johnson's derivation of *sare as* probably a corruption of Arabic *suluhu* does not apply to this meaning.

CHAPTER FOUR

THE IMPORTANCE OF KANGA

Mvua kunya kunya	Rain come down, come down
Mvua kunya kunya	Rain come down, come down
Nitakupa kanga mbili	I will give you two *kangas*.

*K*angas must have been highly regarded by the Waswahili for their children to consider them a gift valuable enough to bring the rain. After all, prayers for rain were given in the public mosques and one of the most beautiful prayers, *du'a*, in the dialect of Sheikh Muhyi'l-Din Al-QaHTany (A.D.1798-1869) the *kadhi,* (Chief Justice) of Zanzibar, was a prayer for rain. The children's treasured gift to capture the rain is *kanga mbili*, a pair of *kanga*.

The *kanga,* an article of clothing worn daily by Waswahili women and men—young and old, modern and traditional, rich and poor, educated and illiterate—has been around for over three hundred years. It is as popular today as it was in the eighteenth century. A woman may own scores of *kangas*, buying a pair whenever a new design comes out, especially if she likes its message. Women inherit *kangas* from their grandmothers. A mother may collect *kangas* for her daughter's wedding long before the proposal has even been made. One summer when I was visiting Zanzibar, a young mother showed me the *kangas* she had been collecting for her daughter's future marriage. The child was only ten years old and not even engaged but mother has to start early as she aims to collect from forty to fifty pairs. Both a child's *somo* (godmother) and the family of the groom present the bride with many pairs of *kanga* as part of her dowry.

From birth to death a female Mswahili is wrapped in a *kanga*. A midwife wraps a baby in a *kanga* as soon as the mother gives birth. When the baby sleeps, a *kanga* serves as a light blanket to cover her up. The child is carried in her mother's arms or on her back in a *kanga*. *Kangas* are associated with her coming of age. Before maturity, a child wears only one *kanga*; her godmother gives her two *kangas* to mark her passage from adolescence to maturity. On marriage, she may share her pair of *kanga* with her husband, each wearing one-half of the pair, the man wearing his like a *shuka or kikoi,* from the waist down, with its message as the lower hem. Both women and men use *kangas* instead of sheets when they cover themselves to sleep. (Figure 14. A girl wearing *kangas*). When a Swahili woman wears two *kangas* in her own home, she wraps one around her body under the armpits so that the written message falls to the ground where it can be seen and read easily. She uses the second *kanga* as a shawl, *mtandio,* to cover her head and shoulders. Again, the writing is at the bottom of the shawl. Elsewhere, as at public gatherings in Tanzania and Kenya, when she is among other women, one *kanga* may serve as a shawl over a western or non-western style dress.

Most importantly, *kangas* cover a woman when she performs her five daily prayers, when she reads the Qurán, or when she recites the *Maulidi* during a celebration of Prophet Muhammad's birthday. Swahili women in East Africa, Oman and other Gulf states cover their heads with a *kanga* when they attend a funeral or *khitma* (wake/mourning). Finally, a pair of new *kangas* is among the cloths that cover a woman when she dies and is prepared for burial. Thus an *Mswahili* woman wears *kangas* daily from birth to death.

Figures 15 to17 show three different ways that two young Swahili women from Zanzibar wear their *kangas*. The *kilemba,* the head cover that we saw being worn by a Swahili woman in the nineteenth century, is still in style two centuries later. Figure 18 shows three women of different age, also from Zanzibar, wearing *kangas* as shawls over modern dresses as they relax at home with relatives and friends. These lightweight fabrics are useful, comfortable, and easy to wear. They constitute the Swahili woman's main costume, an art collection in abundance. She does not employ them as a decoration to adorn her walls or tables; they adorn her body and fill up space in her suitcases, in chests of drawers and on wardrobe shelves. *Kangas* may, indeed, be works of art, material and verbal, but to the owner, even more, a *kanga* serves a practical social function.

Figure 19 shows women celebrating *Kukoga Mwaka* (lit.to bathe the year)*,* an annual bathing ceremony held at Kaekuu in Makunduchi, Zanzibar. The Islamic year is based on a solar agricultural calendar of 365 days. It gets its name from the day of the week on which it begins e.g *Mwaka wa Jummaane*, A Tuesday Year. Historians have called this yearly celebration *Nairuz* and have related it to a Persian ceremony of the same name. *Kukoga Mwaka* is held annually in Zanzibar and Pemba. Women in their beautiful *kangas* move round in a circle singing new songs that recall the social and political events of the past year. They chant: *Mwaka hauna sheria* which means "There is no law on the day that *Mwaka* is celebrated". This is an occasion when quarrels are settled, forgiven, forgotten, and replaced by goodwill. On this day children congregate at their Quränic (Koran) schools early in the morning to walk with their teachers to the sea or a nearby river or well to bathe and wash their writing slates to mark the beginning of the New Year. They sing:

> *Si letu si letu la mwalimu wetu.*
> *Upanga na ngao na kalamu zetu.*
> Not ours, not ours. It [the slate] is our teacher's.
> Sword, shield and pens are ours.

'Sword' and 'shield'stand for defense and protection; the children's pens symbolize their education. Is the message then that education is their defense? A new version of the song substitutes *mbao*, pieces of wood, for *ngao,* shield.

The *Kanga* is a practical garment as far south as Anzuani and Ngazija, the Comoro islands, and as far east as Oman. In the Comoro islands, two pairs of *kangas* may serve as *saluva* or *buibui*, a veil that covers a woman when she goes out of doors. (See Figure 20). In the interior regions of Oman, a woman or young girl away from home wears a *kanga* (*leso*) over her colorful dress or her *l-Haaf*, the shawl that covers her head. Neither the *l-Haaf* nor the *leso* cover the face. The *l-Haaf* is worn instead of a *buibui* or *àbaya*, the black coat-like garment that urban Gulf women and Swahili women wear when they go outdoors. Figure 21 illustrates this style of head-dress. The postcard shows young women from the Sharqiyyah region of Oman carrying a picture of His Majesty Sultan Qaboos bin Said as they celebrate Oman's national day on November18th.[1] In Oman wearing a *leso* over the *l-Haaf* has long been an established form of daily dress.

The *kanga's* attraction for women has continued steadfast to this day. Some women purchase *kangas* from traders and then sell them to other women at a small profit. Every time a new design appears, women without sufficient money to purchase them and those awaiting *kangas* that are not yet in the store, put down a deposit of a shilling or two in order to obtain them later. Some women, because they collect from the trader only some of the newly advertised *kangas* they order, lose their deposits on those they did not collect. In the 1960s some leaders of women associations in Mombasa challenged the disproportionate economic benefit *kangas* brought to Indian merchants. They expressed their anger by leading a boycott when *kanga* prices rose exhorbitantly. A bargain was struck with the merchants. The merchants lowered the deposit women paid on advance orders. Nevertheless the demand continued. The prices remained high. As Mhashamy, one of the boycott organizers put it: "For the question of deposit [on *leso/kanga*], I won. As for the buying of leso, I didn't win"[2].

To this day women sustain the *kanga* business by spending much of their monthly budget on new designs. The current price of a pair of *kangas* in Tanzania is 2500 shillings if they are made locally and 2000 shillings for those made in India. Kenyan *kangas* made of thicker cotton material are the most expensive. They cost 4000 shillings a pair. In Oman, the price for the thinner cotton *kangas* is 1 to 1½ Real (US $ 2.69-4.00). Considering the number of pairs of *kangas* a woman buys in a year, her expenditure on *kangas* is significant.

Although Swahili women are the principle consumers of *kangas,* they are never their manufacturers. Indian and Swahili men import them into Dar es Salaam, Mombasa and Muscat, usually from China, Japan, India or Holland. East Africa and Oman continued to get most of their *kangas* from India, Holland and China at the beginning of the 20th century, but the market changed somewhat after 1962 when the three East African states gained independence from colonial rule. Local companies such as Rivertex of Eldoret in Kenya and Mwatex, Sungura and Urafiki in Tanzania started producing their own *kangas* locally for the East African market. At first local *kangas* were less expensive than those printed abroad. Now, however, those produced in India cost less than those produced in East Africa. By and large, trade and production in cloth, including that in *kangas,* has remained in the control of European and Indian firms to this day.

Cotton originally grew wild in many places on the mainland of Kenya and Tanganyika. It was grown on plantations around Pate, Lamu, Nyanza, Kilwa, Zanzibar and Oman. Burton states that in the nineteenth century English manufactured goods, including cotton piece goods, long cloths and inferior broadcloths were brought to East Africa from India. This confirmed an earlier observation by Owen that two pieces of cloth worn by Congo princesses were manufactured in England.[3] From early travelers' observations we learn that in the fourteenth century Mogadishu in Somalia was a center of cotton manufacture. Women spun the cotton and men wove it. The woven cloth was traded locally along the coast as far as Egypt and the Red Sea. Locally, cloth was used as money and bartered for ivory, gum copal, copra, hides, jute, grains and slaves. In the sixteenth century a Portuguese traveler Barbosa stated that cotton cloth was carried from India to East African markets in *sambuks* sailing first to Mombasa and from there to Sofala, Pemba and Zanzibar. Trade in cloth was also carried out between Usambara, Rufiji, Lindi, and on the islands of Zanzibar and Pemba.

Sadly, the coastal region's economic decline began with the coming of the Portuguese in the sixteenth century. They destroyed the towns, the economy and the peace and tranquility of the Azanian coast. Later European missionaries (beginning with arrival of Krapf of the Church Missionary Society in 1844), colonial merchants and British and German settlers had both good and bad consequences for the politics and economy of the area. The most devastating factor was the introduction of firearms which changed a flourishing and independent economy into a dependent and less prosperous one.

Through commercial relationships with Europe and the United States, East African cotton was exported to the mills of Manchester and Liverpool whereas before cloth had been produced and printed in East Africa itself. It had become the main item of trade with the interior as well as Egypt and the lands bordering the Red Sea.[4] Although cotton was still grown in East Africa in the 1890s, its export was more profitable for European merchants than for the local farmers who cultivated it. Local production declined due to the competition faced from cotton produced in Surat and Kutch in India, from Egyptian and North American cotton and from the British and German control of East African plantations.

Another factor that affected cotton production at that time was the shortage of labor. W.W. Fitzgerald was employed by the Directors of the Imperial British East Africa Company to report on the agricultural capabilities of the coastal plantations. He described several cotton plantations he visited as well as some that he established.[5] He found that:

> Ever since the issue of the Sultan of Zanzibar's Anti- Slavery Decree in 1890, land had been steadily going out of cultivation, a result due, first, to the discouragement caused amongst the Arabs and Swahilis, who are the principal cultivators on the coast, and secondly, to the growing scarcity of slaves; for, by the gradual extension of our [British] influence and stations in the interior, the East African Company was shutting off their usual sources of supply.[6]

The decline in cotton cultivation affected all agricultural products. As for securing labor for the plantations that Fitzgerald himself established, he notes that:

> … we had considerable bother with our labour; the released slaves found that they could earn more by cultivating their own plot of land than by continuing to work on the cotton plantation at the rate of pay we could afford to give them. The Wanika [Wanyika in Kenya] labourers, we found, were always busy on their own plantations at the time we most urgently needed them.[7]

Today, in order to assess anew the market for *kangas,* merchants need to pay attention to purchasers' taste in order to ascertain which *kangas* sell well. They need to know what most attracts sales - designs, colors or sayings. Furthermore, they need to appraise the selling of *kanga bubu* (*kanga* without *jina*) compared with *kanga zenye maandishi*, those that carry *jina*. The government, merchants and buyers should ask themselves, if *kanga* continues to be such a socially valued garment in Eastern Africa and the Arabian Gulf States, would it not be to the economic advantage of these regions to expand local textile technology and redevelop cotton plantations to improve their regional local economies?

Notes

1   I am grateful to photographer Claude Avezard for allowing me to use this picture. Mr. Avezard'sweb page is www. renaizzanze.com.
2. Sara Mirza and M.Stroebel, *Three Swahili Women, Histories from Mombasa* (Kenya, 1989) 92-104. Mhashmy is one of the three Swahili women the authors interviewed for their study.
3. Owen, *Narratives of Voyages (London, 1833)171.*
4. See my discussion earlier on Ibn BaTTuTa's observations.
5. William Walter Fitzgerald discusses the establishment of cotton plantations in different regions of East Africa. See his *Travels in British East Africa Zanzibar and Pemba* (London, 1898) ix.
6. Ibid. 22.
7. Ibid. 639.

CHAPTER FIVE

KANGA MESSAGES

*K*anga inscriptions are a documentary representation of Swahili social and political forms of communication. Here, I examine a random sample of 750 *kanga* names collected over the last two decades. I distinguish and discuss nine categories of *majina*, 'sayings/messages.' These are an important source for understanding Swahili ideal behavior and the Swahili value system; their content relates to both women and men, young and old. They instruct at the same time that they provide an outlet for emotions and expectations. They are a window to changing values and cultural and political attitudes. Sometimes the message portrays what a person may feel but cannot enunciate. Many messages on *kangas* essentially express Swahili women's culture. To men, *kangas* may be simply clothes, garments, to be worn; to women, they speak. Waswahili practice indirect communication which they call *kumpigia mtu fumbo*, casting a riddle for someone. The wearer is expressing a hidden or private message indirectly through the inscription. The message may reach the addressee or may not, but the wearer of the *kanga* has the satisfaction of knowing that she has 'said' it.

Such communications are carefully chosen to capture a mood, express an experience, or convey a hope or warning. Men are not completely oblivious to the messages that surround them; some may, at times, be aware that they refer to them. For example, a woman may buy a pair of *kanga* for herself that says:

Si mzizi si hirizi bali moyo umeridhi
It is due to neither herbal medicine nor an amulet but the heart is willing

(Figure 22) *Mzizi*, a root, is known in local African medicine as *uganga*. *Hirizi*, an amulet, signifies Islamic medicine. It may be made of cloth, leather or metal and contains verses from the Qur'aan. Individuals use both forms of medicine for either protection, cure or gain. A woman wears this *kanga* at a wedding or a wake (*khitma*) to express feelings she wants to share.

If a woman thinks people are jealous, envious or resentful of her relationship with someone, she may buy a *kanga* that says:

Hawatoweza kuizima nuru ya mapenzi yetu
They will not be able to extinguish the light of our love

She may want people to know that she still loves someone by wearing a *kanga* that says:

Mapenzi hayafi
Love never dies (Figure 23.)

On tha *kanga* shown in figure 24, the message reads:

Siri ya mtungi aijuae kata
The ladle knows the secret of the water pitcher

This expresses the idea that a secret is shared only with an intimate. The power of expressing oneself through *kangas* is summed up in the message:

Kanga fimbo ya mwanamke
Kanga is a woman's stick

Parents use sticks to punish or scare children to correcting their behavior. Grown-up men fight with sticks when they have a quarrel, and a woman uses her *kanga's* message as her defense, articulating her apprehension. A fight between two women may arise when the message is deciphered. Such a message may evoke personal emotions and lead those who read it to recollect their own set experiences. Here, perhaps, *kangas* and their messages, besides being communicative weapons, play a role in the process of personality development since they instruct, reinforce and, sometimes, correct the sense of values, social norms or attitudes of those who read them. One such message reads:

Hasira Hasara
Anger is Loss (regret)

This helps build self-control and tolerance by reminding the reader of the disadvantages and weaknesses suffered in resorting to anger. At the same time it discourages angry expressions of feelings. Two simple words carry a deep message.

　　Women who cannot read Roman script often ask their children or others to read a *kanga's* name to them. *Kangas* convey the Waswahili's cultural and literary heritage. Many of the *majina* retain an old verbal tradition but some begin to establish new traditions encapsulating in a particularly pithy and epigrammatic way the social parameters of their wearers' existence. Many convey warm messages, especially when they are used as gifts between relatives and friends. This is expressed in the message on one *kanga* that reads:

Kanga nenda na urembo shani urembo na shani
Kanga, you may go as an adornment, an ornament fine and delicate

As an adornment, a *kanga* is attractive and tasteful. Its message passes on what is valued by the society.

FRIENDSHIP, LOVE AND MARRIAGE

Among the 750 names in my random sample of *kangas* collected between 1984 and 2001, it is possible to distinguish nine categories of *majina*. These are: 1. Friendship, Love and Marriage 2. Hostility and Resentment 3. Family Relationships 4. Wealth and Strength, Cooperation and Competition 5. Patience,

Tolerance and Faith 6. Experience, Knowledge and Action 7. Kindness and Generosity 8. Idd Greetings 9. Politics and National Identity.

The largest category of messages (25.7 percent) refers to friendship, love and marriage. Of its one hundred and ninety three inscriptions, over 92 % (178) apply equally to men and women and may be spoken by either. Examples include:

Pendo letu liwe nono
May our love be strong

Mapenzi ni vitendo sio maneno
Love is actions not words

Duniyani kuna Pepo wawili wapendanapo
There is Heaven on earth when two people love each other

Nakufikiri hutoki moyoni. Nakutamani uje mikononi
I think of you. You are always in my heart. I long for you to be in my arms

Jaraha la moyo haliponi
A broken [wounded] heart does not heal

Si mimi ni moyo
It is not me. It is the heart [talking]

Mapenzi ni nusu ya wazimu
Love drives one almost crazy

Pendo letu ni la dhati
Our love is real

On nineteen *kangas* in this category a third party to a person of either gender is giving advice to lovers. For example,

Umpendae usimfiche siri
Do not hide a secret from the one you love

Usimpende akajua hawachi kujizuzua
Don't love someone to the extent that they know you love them, lest they be conceited

Mpende akupendae
Love the one who loves you

Only eight *majina* names in this category are gender specific

Tai ya Bwana
My husband's bow tie

Akheri Bwana
Good morning, my husband

Cha mumeo chako ringia bahati yako
What belongs to your husband belongs to you. Be proud of your luck

Nakuveka pete yangu uwe mchumba wangu
I am putting a ring on your finger, you are my fiancée

Asmini nimetandika kitandani mimi wako wewe sijui wa nani
I have spread jasmine on the bed. I am yours but I do not know to whom you belong

The message in Figure 25 talks to the husband, reminding him that:

Sifa ya mume ni kupamba mke
A man's reputation lies in the way he adorns his wife

It is utterly wrong to claim, as some have done, that *kangas* and their messages are a uniquely female form of communication. They speak to both sexes about the concerns of both: Friendship is reciprocity. They are about respect for one another, cooperation and sharing, love and pain, action rather than words. Yet they recognize that, with love, there is excitement, uncertainty, doubting, fear and sometimes betrayal. The following *kanga* messages express this feeling of insecurity in relationships.

Nakuridhia kwa kila hali jua nakupenda kweli
You should know that I truly love you because I am attentive to all your needs

Fitina huvunja uhusiano
Intrigue breaks relationships

Si uzuri kutengana
Separation is not good

Niko nawe
I am here with you

Usibadilike
Do not change

Mimi na wewe
You and I

Tusitengane mimi na wewe
You and I should not part

Usiache mbachao kwa msala upitao
Do not give up your straw mat for a passing rug

Mapenzi ni gilasi ikivunjiki basi
Love is like a glass. When it breaks it has vanished

Tulia tuishi wazuri haweshi
Settle down and let us live together, there are so many beautiful people

Nateseka kwa huba
I am suffering because of love

Tulizana mpenzi hakika mimi ni wako
Calm down my beloved. I am truly yours

Wewe ni wangu tu
You are mine

Usinione nacheka moyoni nimeyaweka
Do not see me laughing; I still remember [what has happened]in my heart

Many of these *kanga* messages reflect the fear and reality of separation. All are relevant to and meaningful for both males and females. The next two *kanga* messages are particularly revealing and reflect the changes that have occurred or occurring in marriage relations in Waswahili society.

Ingawa <u>tumeachana</u> yaliobaki ni mazoea
Although we have left one another what is left between us is friendship

Japo <u>umeniacha</u> moyoni hujanitoka
Although you have left me, you are still in my heart

The syntax indicates linguistically a traditional Swahili social structure in which it is the man who divorces while the woman is divorced. In the first of the pair the new structure of the language of the message reflects social change: the reciprocal form of the verb we are divorced (*tumeachana*) replaces you have divorced me (*umeniacha*). The last is said by a woman to her husband. This may be deduced from its syntax – <u>umeniacha,</u> you have left me.

Yet marriage is highly valued, sought after and expected of every young person. Thus we may read:

Harusi ni nguo ya kheri
A wedding is a blessed garment

Harusi ni tamu sote tuwe na hamu
A wedding is sweet (joyful) and we should all look forward to it

Mke wa *nyumbani mwangaza wa chumbani*
A wife in the home is the light in the room

Mke mwema pambo la nyumba
A good wife adorns the home

Mke ni kiungo cha familia
A wife bonds a family

Wawili si mmoja
Two people are not the same as one

In the past, preferred marriages were arranged between girls and their first or second cousins or at least a man of the same kin group. This was not simply for reasons of inheritance keeping property within the family and tracing descent along family lines. It was also a matter of maintaining ethnic or tribal purity and class distinctions. Today, more young people marry persons not of their own tribe or clan, which suggests that girls may choose for themselves their future husbands. Hence, the appearance of new *kanga* messages such as:

Mapenzi hayachagui kabila
Love does not select a lineage

Apendaye chongo huita kengeza
A person in love considers blindness a squint

Nampenda mpenzi wangu mtasema mtachoka hattoki (hatoki)
I love my beloved; you may talk until you are tired but my beloved will not leave me

Niko na wewe mpaka mwisho yakiwa
I'm with you until it happens

Sichagui sibagui anizikaye simjui
I don't choose, I don't discriminate; I don't know who will bury me

Akufaaye kwa dhiki ndiye rafiki
A friend in need is a friend indeed

These days when both husband and wife may work outside the home, it is not uncommon for them to reside at a distance from one another. Because such separation often ends in divorce or marriage to a second wife, men and women pledge reassurances of lasting security:

Powa roho yako mimi wako peke yako
Calm down your heart, I am yours alone

Raha ya moyo wangu mimi kupendwa na wewe
My heart is at peace when you love me

Mimi na wewe pete na kidole
You and I are like a ring and a finger

Kiapo nakuapia mwengine hatatokea
You have my promise; there will be nobody else

They also express the strains of marriage and draw on Islamic tradition instructing couples to separate peacefully. In the Quráan (Koran) Surat 65 on Divorce, verse 2 states: When they have reached their appointed time, then either keep them lawfully or let them go honorably; but have two witnesses among you, and give truthful evidence for God's sake.

A good divorce is better than a bad marriage that makes victims of the children. In modern society where marital dissonance is frequently followed by divorce, several other *kanga* messages convey certain popular expressions mulled over by wives addressing their husbands for example:

Umenitaka kwa kheri tuachane kwa kheri
You wanted me in good faith; let us separate in good faith

Tulia tuishi vizuri
Settle down and let us live in harmony

HOSTILITY AND RESENTMENT

With love, marriage, and divorce comes jealousy, envy, greed, suspicion, hostility, resentment, competition and blame. One hundred and sixty four (21.8 percent of the *kanga* messages in the sample) fall into the category of Hostility and Resentment. These *kanga* messages serve as outlets for complaints or sounding boards for social grievances and accusations that in normal circumstances would be hard to express:

Paka shume mtaani kwenu halahala vitoweo vyenu
A tomcat is in your neighborhood; watch out for your meats [wives or offspring]

Kaa nao lakini ujue tabia zao
Stay with them, but know their habits

Cheka nao ujue tabia zao
Laugh with them so that you may know their ways

Pilipili usozila zinakuashia nini
Why does the hot pepper you have not eaten burn you?

Mchimba kisima huingia mwenyewe
Those who dig wells fall into them

Nia ya shinda [yashinda] kafara
Intention surpasses (is stronger than) a witche's sacrifice

Wache waseme
Let them talk

Wacha udaku
Stop blabbering

Jina langu mpera nifanyalo lawakera
My name is mpera (a guava tree). Whatever I do irritates them

Muwongo mpe chai kwa bakuli aeleze vizuri
Give a liar tea in a large bowl so he may explain things well

Chunga chungio usinichunge mimi siyo mke mwenziyo
Watch over a strainer. Do not watch over (strain) me. I am not your co-wife

Ninaishi kidaktari msemayo natafakari mwisho natowa vidonge vikali
I live like a doctor; I ponder over what you say and in the end I give strong pills

Shika kuta wende msikitini ufisadi si dini
Hold to the walls and go to the mosque. Religion is not a vice

Ninakuoneya huruma. Sijuwi nikwambie
I feel sorry for you. I do not know whether I should confide in you (or not)

Sitobadili pendo langu kwa jambo la kusikia
I will not change my love because of rumours

Mapenzi ni vitendo sio maneno
Love is actions not words

Jaraha la moyo haliponi
A wounded (broken) heart does not heal

Wapende wao wakipenda wenzao huwa mwao
It is all right when they fall in love, but it is a big thing when others do

Gossip and, at the same time, fear of words is apparent from these messages. Waswahili are sensitive to what is said of them and several *kanga* state that words cause more harm to the heart than a blow. Love is actions not words. In a marriage a wife should be punished by words not blows. Thus:

Mke hapigwi kwa fimbo hupigwa kwa maneno
A wife is not to be hit with a cane, but should be punished with words

Out of the one hundred and forty nine messages in this category, thirteen talk about gossiping, twelve about envious persons, twelve about *fitina,* a troublemaker or seductive individual, and five about minding your own business:

Bora kujikwaa dole kuliko ulimi
It is better to trip with your toe than with your tongue

Usiniseme
Do not gossip about me

Mola tunusuru midomo ya waja isitudhuru
God protect us so we are not harmed by what people say

Kumezea ni kawaida yangu kwa kuwa sipendi majungu
Endurance is my custom because I do not like conspiring

Mimi kawaida yangu Sijui wewe limbukeni
For me it is my custom. I do not know about you, the novice

Ulijuwaje kama si umbea
How did you know that if it were not through prying?

Uncertainty in social relations leads to reliance on sorcery or witchcraft, *uchawi or uganga*. This may have various objectives: protecting from harm or gain in marriage or to further a relationship or a career, or a cure. The dangers of this mode of relieving uncertainty or anxiety is recognized in several messages, e.g.:

Si mzizi si hirizi bali moyo umeridhi
It is neither because of herbal medicine nor my amulet, my heart is willing

Dawa ya penzi ni penzi
The medicine of love is love [i.e. not witchcraft]

Si mzizi ni bahati yangu
It is not a root (witchcraft). It is my luck

Waganga mtamaliza mimi hamtaniweza
You will go to all the witch doctors in turn, but you will do me no harm

Today one may encounter a few negative *kanga* names that are out of keeping with traditional civility and courtesy. This has led to a call for censorship and control over *kanga* names. Until that occurs, a *kanga* with an improper message may be rejected, ignored or trigger an even nastier response. One *kanga* read:

Chakubimbi ukimwona mwogope
You should be afraid of a rumor-monger when you see one

To which another *kanga* responded:

Chakubimbi mamako
The rumor-monger is your mother

That message goes beyond the bounds of expected behavior. Degrading someone's mother is the greatest insult in Swahili culture. Other impolite messages include:

Kila waonalo wasema na hili pia kaseme
You tell about every thing that you see, so go and tell about this one

Mmesahau kazi zenu kutwa kunisengenya
You have forgotten your work while you scandalize me all day long

Wameshindwa wenye meno utayaweza wewe kibogoyo
Those with their own teeth could not succeed let alone you who is toothless

We! Kinyau nyau kikiya cha pweza
You! A little kitten with the small tail of an octopus

Men and women who complain about these recent 'non-traditional expressions' view the function of *kangas* to be that of bearing sociable, educational and instructive messages, not insults. In turning away from them, some women look instead for *kanga bubu, kangas* that have no message of any kind and therefore do not speak. Subsequently, several *kangas* without messages have appeared in Oman as seen in.Figures 26-28. This is to be deplored. Eliminating names from *kangas* because of a few negative messages that have surfaced is counter productive and fails to recognize the social importance of *kanga* messages as a literary and educational source. There are also some young women who find entertainment and satisfaction in wearing *kanga* carrying these modern messages.

FAMILY RELATIONSHIPS

Out of 750 messages ninety-three (12.3 percent) are about parents and their children. Of these nearly half (i.e. 45.6 percent) specifically mention the mother. Although this is a strongly patrilineal Islamic society women are valued through these messages. These convey an attitude that there is no one like a mother, that a mother's blessings and prayers are better than worldly wealth. A mother likes to see her child happy and protected and the child prays to resemble her. Islam teaches obedience to the mother. Heaven lies at the feet of the mothers or in Arabic, 'Aljannatu taHta aqdaami-l-ummahaat.' This is reiterated in the *kanga* message that says:

Pepo yako chini ya miguu ya mama yako
Your heaven lies at your mother's feet

Many *kangas* articulate unambiguously this sentiment. For example,

Hakuna kama mama
There is no one like mother

Nani kama mama
What other person is like a mother?

Radhi ya mama yashinda mali ya dunia
A mother's blessing is better than worldly wealth

Maziwa ya mama ni bora
Mother's milk is best

Mama awe chambo cha haki duniani
Let your mother be your source of justice in your world

Mama hana kijicho
A mother does not envy her child

Moyo unafurahika mama akiona mtoto kasitirika
A mother is happy when she sees her child well protected

Nikulipe nini mama[1]
Mother, how can I repay you?

Nikupe zawadi gani mama
My mother, what present should I give you?

Nimpe zawadi gani mama
What present should I give my mother?

Nimetembea kila pembe namtafuta nani kama mama
I have searched in every corner looking for someone like my mother

Radhi ya mama ni neema
Mother's blessing is a comfort

Mama yangu mpenzi kumkosa siwezi
My dearest mother, I cannot do without her

Siwezi kuishi bila wewe mama
Mother, I cannot live without you

Sifa ni ya mama mlezi
The compliments are for the mother who raises the child

Uchungu wa mwana aujuaye mzazi
It is the one who gives birth who knows the pain of child bearing

Hakuna mlezi amshindaye mama
No foster parent takes the place of a mother

Mama nambari wani hana mpinzani
Mother is number one; no one can compete with her

Mama ni dhahabu kwa mema aliyonitendea
A mother is as precious as gold for the good she has done for me

Mama ni dhahabu haistahili kumpa adhabu
Mother is precious as gold, she does not deserve suffering

Mzazi ni mzazi kumtupa siwezi
A parent is a parent. I cannot set her aside

A mother's responsibility in caring for her husband and her children and the heavy burden she carries in maintaining the family is spelt out in the following *kanga* messages:

Mke mwema pambo la nyumba
A good wife adorns the home

Mke mwema ni ua nyumbani huchanua
A good wife is a flower that blooms in the home

Radhi ya mume ni Pepo
A wife gets to heaven through her husband's blessings

Furaha ya mume ni pepo
A husband's happiness is bliss
A husband's happiness brings heaven to his wife

Mke ni nguo
A wife is a garment

Only ten of the ninety-three sayings mention both parents. Parents are blessed when their children please them and when children obey their parents they gain their blessings. These *kangas* say:

Usisahau wazazi
Do not forget your parents

Mimi nimekiri mapenzi ya wazee wawili
I have acknowledged the love of two parents

Neema ya wazee furaha ya watoto
The comfort of parents lies in their children's joy

Respecting your parents, listening to them, pleasing them and obeying them gain you their blessings and their love that brings peace to the family. Five *kanga* messages stress the importance of the blessings the children will receive if they please their parents.

Ukiridhi wazazi utapata radhi
If you obliged your parents, you will receive their blessings

Ukifurahisha wazazi utapata radhi
If you please your parents, you will be blessed

Shika ya wazazi upate radhi
Hold to what your parents say so that you may be blessed

Wazazi nawaenzi nipate radhi (za) Mwenyezi
I respect my parents in order to get God's blessings

Wazazi nawaenzi nipate radhi
I respect my parents in order to get blessings

The Qurán lays down this guidance:

> So your Lord has decreed: Do not worship anyone but him, and be good
> to your parents.If one or both of them grow old in your presence, do not
> say fie to them, nor reprove them, but say gentle words to them. And look
> after them with kindness and love, and say : Ö Lord, have mercy on them
> as they cared for me when I was a little child." (17:22-24)

The blessings of parents nourish the child and the prayers of a son or daughter are considered important to the parents. Their reciprocal responsibility strengthens the family. Good nurturing is essential for both parents and children.

Today paradoxically, many children are raised by foreign housemaids and nannies. They come from different cultures and speak different languages from that of the family. Consequently, the role of parents in raising their own children receives specific mention. *Kangas* sold in the last ten years are specific about the correct upbringing of children. Parents should raise their children, sons and daughters should respect and obey their parents. A wife is responsible for her children, her husband and her home, but the feelings and opinions she expresses on the *kangas* she wears affect her children's attitudes and her husband's decisions.

Wazazi walio wema wajua manufaa ya watoto
Good parents know what is good for their children

Mimba si kazi; kazi kulea mwana
Carrying a pregnancy is not hard work but raising the child is

Udongo uwahi ulimaji
Mould the clay while it is still damp

Mwana umleavyo ndivyo akuavyo
The way you raise the child is the way he will grow

Mcha mwana kulia hulia yeye
The parent who is afraid of the child crying, that parent will end up crying

Kicheko cha mtoto ni furaha kwa wazazi
The child's laughter is the parents' happiness

Ukali wa jicho washinda wembe
An eye is sharper than a razor blade

Asiyesikia la mkuu huvunjika guu
He who does not listen to his elder's word breaks his leg

Mchezea wembe humkata mwenyewe
He who plays with a razor blade cuts himself

Malezi mema muongozo wa dunia
A good upbringing nurtures one through life

All these *kanga* messages express the idea that the family, and especially the mother in the family, plays an important role in nurturing a child.. The home unit today usually consists of father, mother and their children living apart from aunties, uncles and grandparents. Reliance on foreign maids is extreme.

The strong emphasis placed on a mother's role and love has become a form of self-defense for women. It is also a strategy in a society where, after a divorce, a woman who remarries may lose the custody of her son when he attains at the age of seven or a daughter when she reaches puberty. Because society stigmatizes women who take their complaints to court, *kanga* sayings voice such a mother's distress.

WEALTH AND STRENGTH, COOPERATION AND COMPETITION

Feelings of ownership, possession and contentment are portrayed in the messages which appear in this fourth category: Wealth and Strength, Cooperation and Competition. These seven messages claim health and contentment to material wealth.

Bora ni afya si mali
Health is better than wealth

Pesa fitina ya binadamu
Money is man's affliction

Utajiri wa moyo ni bora kuliko fedha
A contented heart is better than wealth

Nakiri wangu umaskini siombi wala siazimi
I acknowledge that I am poor but I do not beg or borrow

Radhi ni bora kuliko mali
Blessing is better than wealth

Mapenzi ni mali ya moyo
Love is the wealth of the heart

Kutoa ni moyo
Giving requires a heart

Both health and blessings are valued above wealth, but poverty is seen as a handicap:
Dau la mnyonge halendi joshi
A poor man's boat does not sail smoothly

Bora kupata kuliko kukosa
Getting something is better than losing. [Something is better than nothing]

Kingi cha kungojea si kidogo cha kupokea
The little you receive is better than that for which you have to wait

Waswahili are advised to emulate the busy honey-producing bees:

Fuata nyuki ule asali
Follow bees so you may eat honey

Pesa huzaa pesa
Money produces money

But, at the same time, they are cautioned of the rage of the bee:

Nyuki mkali kwa asali yake
A bee is fiercely protective of its honey

They are advised to be self-reliant and not to depend on relatives. Nineteen out of the sixty-seven names promote contentment with what one has.

Mtumai cha ndugu hufa hali masikini
He who relies on inheriting a relative's property dies poor

Nguo ya kuazima haisitiri matako
A borrowed garment does not cover one's behind

Tengeneza chako usahau cha mwenzako
Fix what belongs to you and forget someone else's

Usisafirie nyota ya mwenzio
Do not be guided. Follow your own star

Ingawa masikini moyo wangu tajiri
Although I am poor, my heart is rich

Hohe hahe ana siku yake
A destitute man has his (lucky) day

Bora umaskini wangu kuliko utajiri wako
My poverty is better than your wealth

Kibaya changu si chema cha mwenzangu
An ugly thing that is mine is better than the beautiful thing of another

Nala yangu riziki siwajali wanafiki
I eat what God has given me. I do not pay attention to hypocrites

Popote nilipo na raha
I am comfortable wherever I am

Niliyotamani nishapata
I have what I have longed for

Reading between the lines, the following messages discourage avid competition for possession.

Usimwingilie aliyepewa kapewa
He who has been given has been given. Do not interfere with him
He who has has

Vuta nkuvute yararua nguo
You're pulling and I'm pulling. It tears the garment

Wapiganapo tembo nyasi huumia
When elephants fight, the grass gets hurt

Wealth has its advantages and seeking it through business is acceptable, but one must be aware of the slippery path of greed that may lead to loss. The following *kanga* sayings contrast wealth and the lack of it, putting both in their right perspective:

Njaa mwanamalegeza shibe mwana malevya
Hunger weakens a person, but satiation intoxicates him

Kupata si uerevu na kukosa si ujinga
Getting is not being clever and losing is not being ignorant

Ufukara si kilema
Poverty is not disability

These sayings reflect on and instruct against a prevalent attitude at a time when desire for ownership is becoming paramount. In affluent times when money and wealth seem to buy anything and everything, some women are expressing discontent with materialistic gifts from a suitor and are asking for real love and decent treatment:

Simuhitaji wa dhahabu wala fedha muhitaji wa mapenzi ukiweza
I am in need of neither gold nor silver; I need love if you are capable of giving it to me

Maneno matamu hulainisha moyo mgumu
Sweet words soften a hard heart

Maneno matamu pumbazo la moyo
Sweet words comfort the heart

Kauli njema yashinda tajiri [utajiri]
Kind words are better than wealth

Moyo wangu sultani cha mtu sikitamani
My heart is like that of a sultan; I do not envy what anyone else has

Shingo huvaa vyombo roho huvaa mambo
The neck wears jewelry; the soul wears problems

Bora umaskini wangu kuliko utajiri wako
My poverty is better than your wealth

Ingawa masikini moyo wangu tajiri
Although I am poor, my heart is rich

Sumu ya mahaba ni nini
What is the poison of love?

Haki ya mtu hailiki
A person's rights cannot be consumed by someone else

Kaamil alawsaaf 'atinii diinaar
Most just person, give me a dinaar

The dinaar is a coin used in parts of Arabia and this last *kanga* saying is printed in Arabic, not Swahili. In the last two messages, wealth is linked to just behavior.

PATIENCE, TOLERANCE AND FAITH

Patience, tolerance and reliance on God are values in daily discourse. Out of 750 names, sixty-one of them (8.3 percent) fall into this category. In eight out of sixty-one (13.1 percent), the speaker is asking for *subira* (patience). In 1984-86 alone four different designs appeared in Oman with a similar message:

Subira ufunguo wa Peponi
Patience is the key to Heaven

Subira ni njema
Patience is good

Subira miftahu al-khayr
Patience is the key to good

Subira huleta mafanikio
Patience brings success

Three *kangas* with similar messages appeared in Zanzibar at the same time:

Subira ni njema
Patience is good

Yailahi Nipe Moyo wa Subira
God give me a patient heart

Subira ni mali kwa mwenye kuwa nae (nayo)
Patience is wealth for he who has it

Others state:

Baada ya dhiki faraji
Consolation comes after distress

Kila mwenye kusubiri mola hatomuadhiri
God does not disgrace the one who is patient

Mwenye pupa hadiriki kula tamu
A hasty person does not have the time to eat a ripe fruit

Ya nini wivu. Mstahmilivu hula mbivu
Why are you jealous? The one who is patient eats ripe fruit

Simba mwenda kimya ndiye mla nyama
A quiet lion is the one that eats the meat

Subiri upate mradi wako
Be patient so you may get what you desire

A *kanga* from Kenya says:

Subira huleta mafanikio
Patience brings success

Similarly, a *kanga* from Tanzania reiterates:

Siupi moyo wasiwasi mwenye kusubiri hakosi
I do not allow doubts into my heart. A patient person is not at a loss

Patience is necessary if an individual is to maintain harmonious relationships in a society that values social communication. Another value attached to patience is the ability to endure or tolerate. Six *kanga* messages convey this:

Tua kwanza
First, calm down

Raha haiji ila baada ya taabu
Comfort does not come except after some difficulty

Mwenda pole haumii mguu
The one who walks slowly does not hurt his leg

Usione namezea. Ugomvi sikuzoea
You see me swallowing. I am not used to quarreling

Kumeza ni kawaida yangu kwa kuwa sipendi majungu
My habit is tolerance (swallowing) since I do not like conspiring

Patience and tolerance are accompanied by faith in divine mercy and trust that things will be better tomorrow. Faith in the divine gives a person strength to endure and courage to go on. Like any other religion, Islam encourages tolerance and reliance on God.

Tawakkal 'alaa llah inna llaha yuHibbu lmutawakkiliyn
Depend on God for God likes those who depend on him

Two different *kanga* designs both bear the saying:

Mpaji ni Mungu
The giver is God.[You are not in full control, God is]

Other *kanga* sayings that relate to God tell us that:

Sisi sote abiria dereva ni Mungu
We are all passengers; the driver is God

Lolote likupatalo limeandikwa na Mungu
Whatever befalls you, God has ordained it

Ulipendalo hupati hupaata ujaliwalo
You do not get what you like; you get what God has destined for you

Apendalo Mungu haliwezekani
No one can undo what God wishes

Shukuru Mungu
Be grateful to God

Ukipata shukuru
Be grateful when you get something

Nashukuru kwa yote
I am grateful for everything

Gratitude to God combines with hope:

Jaza yako iko kwa Mungu
Your reward is with God

Hohe hahe ana siku yake
Even a poor man has his good day

Mtaka yote kwa pupa hukosa yote
He who wants all in haste loses all

Chembe na chembe ni mkate
A grain and another grain make a loaf

Kiinga na kinga ndipo moto huwaka
A stick and another stick, the fire burns

Kheri kenda shika kama kumi nenda uje
Holding nine now is better than holding ten later
(A bird in the hand is worth ten in the bush.)

With such advice, burdens become bearable and people blame themselves less. See also Figure 29. Out of the sixty sayings in this category only twelve focus specifically on faith as a doctrine. Most refer to values and a way of life integrally connected with faith.

Usimsahau mola wako ndiye atowae riziki
Do not forget your Lord. He is the one who provides sustenance

Imani huwa ni moyoni haiwi mdomoni
Faith is in the heart not on the lips

Mwenye dini hakosi imani
He who has religion has faith

Imani ya mtu imo ndani ya roho yake
One's faith is in one's heart

Sitaki raha ya dunia. Nataka raha ya kesho
I do not want the comfort of this world. I want the comfort of the next

Mola nisitiri
Lord, protect me

Mtupie Mungu kilio sio binaadamu mwenzio
Address your cry to God, not your fellow human being

Aliyenipa Mola wangu huizuwii riziki yangu
You cannot stop my good fortune; my Lord has given it to me

Kumcha Mungu ni mwanzo wa hekima
Fear of God is the beginning of wisdom

Usife moyo mwenyezi Mungu yupo
Do not lose hope; there is God

Penye wengi pana Mungu
Where people are gathered together there is God

> *Mungu nijaalie mabaya yasinifikie*
> God protect me from evilness

Good fortune becomes part of the unseen and the unpredictable that is destined by the Creator. Several sayings express belief in the benefit of good fortune.

> *Bahati ni mali*
> Luck is wealth

> *Nategemea bahati yangu situmaini cha mtu*
> I rely on my luck. I do not depend on what belongs to another

Bahati gets you a good job; it gives you status and wealth and brings you friends and marriage. Lack of *bahati* deprives you of these things. It usurps your strength and consequently your success. It might lead you to doing nothing.

> *Imani ninayo bahati sina*
> I have faith but not luck

> *Aso bahati habahatiki*
> One who is not fortunate does not benefit from luck

> *Usisafirie nyota ya mwenzio*
> Do not travel by someone else's star. (Follow your own course)

> *Bahati ikenda kombo mwerevu huwa mjinga*
> When luck becomes skewed, an intelligent person becomes unintelligent

> *Maskini wa bahati tajiri wa matatizo*
> (I am) poor in luck and rich in problems

Anyone can be lucky:

> *Bahati haina kwao*
> Luck is homeless

Many sayings recognize weakness and encourage passivity:

> *Mimi nyumba ya udongo sihimili vishindo*
> I am a mud hut. I cannot endure blows

> *Usishindane na wenye bahati*
> Do not compete with the lucky ones

> *Mwenye nguvu mpishe*
> Let the strong one pass

Adui mpende
Love thy enemy

Many encourage bravery and daring:

Naogopa simba na meno yake. Siogopi mtu kwa maneno yake
I am afraid of a lion's teeth. I am not afraid of a person's words

Usitake ushindani huniwezi asilani
Do not compete with me; you will not win

Again concern over what others say to a person or about a person, is challenged in the saying:
Siogopi mtu kwa maneno yake
I am not afraid of a person because of what he says

EXPERIENCE, KNOWLEDGE AND ACTION

The sixth category of sixty-one messages (8 percent of the sample) addresses experience, knowledge and right action in accomplishing what one sets out to do. These messages emphasize the importance of planning and thinking before acting and of learning from experience. These say:

Mambo kwa bongo
*All m*atters require brain

Dunia ni maarifa
The world is an experience

Hayataki nguvu mambo ni ujuzi
All matters require knowledge not strength

Mpanda ovyo hula ovyo
Careless sowing leads to careless harvesting
(As you sow so, you will reap)

Apandae [apandaye] huvuna
He who plants will harvest

Fikiri kabla hujasema
Think before you speak

Fikiri kwanza ndipo uamue
Think first and then decide

Kuuliza si ujinga
Asking does not show ignorance

These sayings call for thinking before acting and prompt action as well as the realization that there are many ways of accomplishing anything.

Utu ni kitendo chema
Humanity is doing a good deed

Muungwana hajinadi huonyesha vitendo
An honorable person does not brag. He acts

Mchele moja (mmoja) mpishi mwingi[mapishi mengi]
There may be one kind of rice but there are several ways of cooking it

Kila chombo kwa wimbili
Every seagoing vessel makes it wake

Maneno yawe mafupi vitendo viwe virefu
Let the words be short and the actions long

Si hoja maneno bora vitendo
Actions are better than words

Vishindo vingi sio kutenda jambo
Too much commotion is the same as inaction

Usipoziba ufa utajenga ukuta
Unless you fill the crack, you will have to rebuild the entire wall

Ukitaja nyoka shika kigongo
If you refer to a snake, be prepared with a stick (talk of the devil)

Kwenda mbio si kufika
Running is not arriving

Age commands respect and is associated with experience, wisdom and knowledge. The young are expected to consult their elders and to respect and obey their opinions. Yet, surprisingly, perhaps, only a few *kanga* messages reflect this cultural value. These include:

Udongo wa zamani siyo wa sasa
Today's clay is not the same as yesterdays

Jungu kuu halishi koko, (ukoko)
A big cooking pot is never without burnt bits sticking to it

Usidharau tawi matunda yanapostawi
Do not ignore the branch when the fruits on the tree are flourishing

Asiyesikia la mkuu huvunjika guu
He who does not listen to an elder's word will break his leg

Because wealth and good health may derive from good luck and destiny, friends and relatives are given *kangas* that carry prayers asking for good luck, blessings and peace.

Nakuombea dua
I am praying for you

Mungu akupe baraka na mie nifurahi
May God grant you his blessings and I will be happy

Mwenyezi Mungu akuzidishie kila la kheri
May the Almighty God bless you with everything that is good

Mwenyezi Mungu akupe baraka na mie nifurahi
May the Almighty God bless you and I will be happy

Mungu akupe furaha na amani maishani
May God give you happiness and peace in your life

Dua njema kwako mpenzi
This beautiful prayer is for you, my dear

KINDNESS AND GENEROSITY

People generally admire a kind and generous person who brings joy and abhors causing misery. Kindness and generosity are reflected in forty-four (i.e.6 percent) of the *kanga* sayings in the sample. For one example see Figure 30.

Akufaaye ndiye rafiki
He who is of help to you is indeed a friend

Akufaaye kwa dhiki ndiye rafiki
He who helps you while you are in distress is a real friend
A friend in need is a friend indeed

Utu ni kitendo chema
Humanity is a good deed

Hisani haiyozi
Kindness does not go bad

Wema hauozi
Goodness does not go bad

Heri jema
Goodness is better

Furaha yako faida kwangu
Your happiness is my gain

Furaha yako ni yangu
Your happiness is mine

Tumkirimu mgeni
Let us be hospitable to the guest

Kikubwa sina. Kidogo Pokea
I do not have a big gift. Receive this small one

Usikumbuke uovu ukasahau fadhila
Do not dwell on the bad and forget the kindness

Sitosahau fadila (fadhila) kwa dhiki ya mara moja
I will not forget kindness on account of a brief distress

Zawadi ni dawa. Hupoza hasira
A gift is medicine. It cools down anger

Zawadi ni chochote kupokea usichoke
Anything is a gift. Do not be tired of one

Mwenye roho njema hufaidi duniani.
He who has a good heart benefits in this world

Naja na heri mwenye nyumba hodi
Owner of the house, may I come in. I am bringing good fortune

Mwenyezi Mungu akuzidishie kila la kheri
May the Almighty God increase your blessings

Nia njema ni tabibu nia mbaya huharibu
A good intention is a cure, a bad intention is harmful

Kindness is reciprocal and leads to cooperation.

Mkono mmoja hauchinji ng'ombe
One hand does not slaughter a cow

Mkono mmoja haupigi kofi
One hand does not clap

Kidole kimoja hakivunji chawa
One finger cannot crush a louse

Wawili si mmoja
Two people are not one

Chako chetu
Yours is ours

Furaha yako ni faida yangu
Your happiness is my gain

Ingawa kidogo hisani sitasahau
Although it may be a small thing I will never forget a kindness

Halahala jirani japo ni baniyani
Take care of a neighbor even if he is a Hindu [of a Banyan trading caste]

In the previous discussion I suggested that *kanga* messages are a reflection of their times. As times change, so do the cultural values expressed on *kangas*.

IDD GREETINGS

This category of messages consists of forty messages (5.3 per cent of all those in the sample) that appear seasonally. These convey *Idd salaams*, "greetings". Idd greetings on *kangas* are the equivalent of seasonal greeting cards in other parts of the world. They appear twice a year, first during Idd el-FiTr (the holiday that is celebrated after the fasting month of Ramadhan) and then Idd el-Hajj (celebrated at the end of the pilgrimage season to Mecca). Several *kanga* designs with the same or similar messages are sold before an Idd festival. For example Figures 31 and 32. This category includes the following:

Eid Mubarak
Idd Blessing

Pokea mkono wa Eid
Accept my Idd Greetings

Sikukuu ya furaha
Happy Idd

Mpenzi wangu pokea mkono wa Idd
My dear, accept my Idd greetings

Furaha ya Idd shukuru Mola
For Idd happiness be thankful to God

Yarabi tupe furaha kwa siku hii ya Iddi
God grant us happiness on this Idd day

Salam ya Idd mpe umpendae
Give Idd greetings to the one you like/love

Pokea Iddi mpenzi upate kunienzi
Receive this Idd my dear, think highly of me

Pokea zawadi ya Idd uzidi kunienzi
Receive this Idd present so you may think more highly of me

Nakuomba iwe Idi ya kheri
I beg you (Lord), let it be a good Idd

Idd Mubarak mwakani twende Makka
Idd greetings. Let us go to Mecca next year

Hongera ya Idd mubarak
Congratulations on a happy Idd

These *kanga* messages convey Idd greetings from the giver to the receiver. There are also those that respond to a greeting or gift that has been received:

Ahsante kwa zawadi ya siku hii ya Iddi
Thank you for this Idd present

Umenifurahisha hadi kunikumbuka siku ya Idd
You have made me happy by remembering me on Idd day

Ewe Mola wetu na iwe sherehe ya furaha kwetu
O our Lord, make it a happy celebration for us

Salamu ya Idd kutoka kwa mpenzi wangu
(Thanks for) Idd greetings from my beloved

Kangas not only form the main item of gift exchange between relatives and friends at Idd. They also constitute a productive business for traders during the two *Idd* seasons. The messages reappear the following year with different designs and slightly changed words. At other times popular messages also repeat. Two different designs may appear with the same message for example:

Akili ni mali
Wisdom is wealth

In 1986 two *kangas*, one printed for Zanzibar and the other for Oman had different designs but bore the same message:

Hisani huna na fadhila hukumbuki
You are not kind and you do not remember gratitude

POLITICS AND NATIONAL IDENTITY

The ninth category consists of twenty-four names (3.2 percent) about politics and national identity. These *kangas* began to appear in Tanzania amid political party campaigns in the early 1960s. The idea caught on after Tanzania gained its independence from Britain in 1962 and after the union of mainland Tanganyika with the islands of Zanzibar and Pemba in 1964. Some of these messages are very general:

Faida ya wananchi kuijenga nchi
For the benefit of citizens, build the country

Burudika moyo wako ujenge taifa lako
Cool down your heart and build your nation

Tusisahau kwetu
Let us not forget our homeland

Uno na uno nitunde upi
This one and that one, which [party] do I choose?

Muokoa nchi ndio mwananchi
The citizen is the one who saves the country

Others specifically commemorate key events in national history:

Twalipenda Azimio la Arusha
We like the Arusha Declaration

Saba Saba ya ishirini na mbili, 1976 Tanzania
1976 is the twenty-second anniversary of TANU [the Tanganyika African National Union]

Azimio la Arusha
Arusha Declaration

Sikizana na wenzio ujenge ujamaa
Get along with your friends to build familyhood (Tanzanian socialism)

In 1992 Zanzibar began to place emphasis on new goals:

Kinasema chama chetu kilimo msingi wetu
Our political party says that farming is our foundation

Utekelezaji ndio wajibu wetu kuijenga nchi yetu
Achievement is our duty to build our country

Uchumi wa nchi ndio maendeleo yetu
The country's economic earnings are our progress

New sayings instruct citizens to develop their country, to build their new nation and to strengthen the economy by working cooperatively within a system of *Ujamaa*, Tanzanian socialism. This will bring them love, unity and peace which can only be achieved by getting along with others in their community, "*Sikizana na wenzio ujenge ujamaa.*" Get along with your friends in order to build familyhood. (See Figure 33). They are also reminded of "*Azimio la Arusha*", the independence declaration that set out the goals of the new government. These *kangas* are the products of the time.

The 1990s was also a period when numerous emigrants continued moving to Oman for a better life, after the 1963's revolution in Zanzibar. Thus Oman contributes some national messages. They include:

Uishi wapi
Where should you live?

Hapo ni kwako
This place is your home

' Umaan aSli wa faSliy
Oman my origin and my family

Omani amani
Oman is peaceful

'Uman al-yawm
Today's Oman

ArDuna aTTayyiba 'aashat
Long live our beautiful land

Kupendana amani na umoja
Love, peace and unity

Kupendana Amani na Umoja ni uamuzi
Love, Peace and Unity is the choice

Photographs

Figure 1: Kisutu

Figure 2: Swahili 19-Century woman wearing a dress made out of a kanga.

Figure 3: Kukopa furaha kulipa matanga (in Arabic script)

Figure 4: Wema hauozi

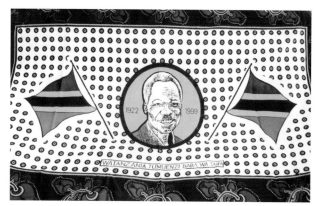

Figure 5: Julius Nyerere 1922-1999

Figure 6: Jogoo ZNP symbol

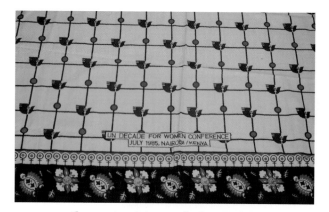

Figure 7: UN Decade for women

Figure 8: Salama Salimina

Figure 9: AlHamdulillah Àssalaama

Figure 10: Oman Coffee Pot

Figure 11: Kanga at Darajani Street

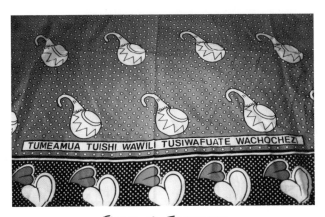

Figure 12: Tumeamua

Figure 13: Women wearing Kangas at a shower party in Boston

Figure 14: A Zanzibar child wearing Kangas

Figures 15 - 16: Two styles in wearing a pair of Kanga

Figure 18: Three Zanzibar women in their kangas

Fig 17: Kanga worn as a headdress

Figure 19: Mwaka Celebration

Figure 20: In Comoro kanga worn as saluva

Figure 21: Oman National Day

SI MZIZI SI HIRIZI BALI MOYO UMERIDHI

Figure 22: Si mzizi

MAPENZI HAYAFI

Figure 23: Mapenzi hayafi

Figure 24: Siri ya Mtungi

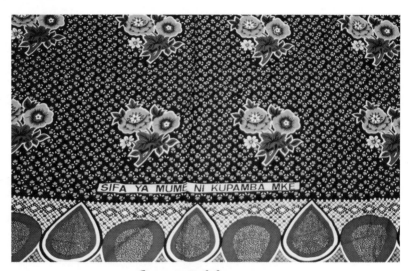

Figure 25: Sifa ya mume

Figure 26: Kanga bubu

Figure 27: Kanga bubu

Figure 28: Kanga bubu

Figure 29: Mungu nijaalie

Figure 30: Akufaaye ndiye rafiki

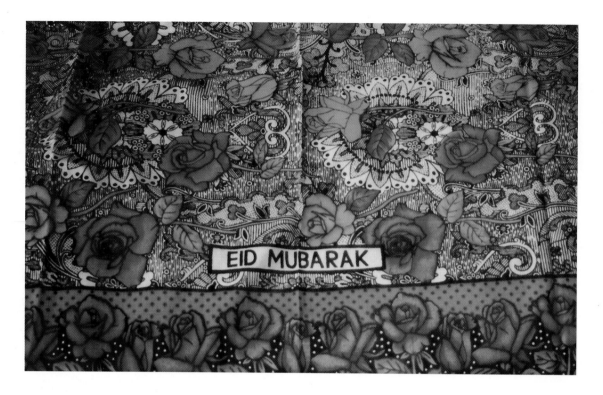

Figure 31: Eid Mubarak

Figure 32: Eid Mubarak

Figure 33: Sikilizana na wenzio

Figure 34: A mutilated kanga

Figure 35: Hello Good morning

Figure 36: Akili ni mali

Figure 37: Nadiymu-l-qalb

Figure 38: Fort Nakhl

Figure 39: Oman al-yawm

Figure 40: An Omani dress with l-Haaf

SawTu l-nahDa
Let voices awaken

Some of these expressions recall the migration of Waswahili from East and Central Africa to Oman in 1970's and 1990's when many Waswahili gained or regained Omani nationality. They settled in Oman and became Omanis. The last saying is in Arabic and it commemorates Oman's fifteenth National Day.

MESSAGES STRENGTHEN SOCIO-CULTURAL VALUES

Majina the messages on *kangas* perform several different functions. They introduce new concepts, give expression to feelings and serve as reminders of events. They are teaching devices. They teach the young and remind the old of the behavior expected of them. One *kanga* says:

Mwana mtulivu haambiwi mara mbili
An attentive child is not told something twice

A dependable person does not have to be constantly reminded of his or her obligation. As we have seen, the role of the mother in raising her children and affecting their behavior and development is considered important in the wellbeing of a family and society. If she does not perform this obligation, the child will learn good and bad from those around him.

Asiyefunzwa na mamaye hufunzwa na ulimwengu
He who is not taught by his mother is taught by the world

Dunia ni maarifa
The world is an experience

Knowledge of the world expands one's experience. One learns from the world that life is not a bed of roses but of seed-bed edifying experiences.

Mpiga ngumi ukuta huumiza mkonowe
He who strikes the wall hurts his hand

The idea that violence injures its perpetrator has been recaptured and recast by Ebrahim Hussein, a famous Tanzanian playwright, in his play *Wakati Ukuta* (Time is a Wall) first published in 1967. In Hussein's play, Asha, the mother, is fighting against the changes that are brought with time. She is hurt when her daughterTatu runs away with a boy friend, Swai. Tatu suffers because she does not listen to her mother's instructions and consequently makes a bad marriage that ends in an unanticipated divorce. Hussein's play depicts the conflict between the young and old, between modern and traditional times.
Several *kanga* provide advice for the younger generation. For example,

Mtaka cha mvunguni sharti ainame
He who wants to get something from under the bed must stoop for it

Jicho la mzazi ni bunduki
The parent's eye is a gun

Mbiyo za sakafuni huishiya ukingoni
Running across the roof of a house brings to its edge

Mkaidi hafaidi ila siku ya Iddi
A stubborn person is not repaid until Idd day

This last message is often said to children. The child is reminded of his mischievousness or stubbornness on *Idd* day if he does not receive a gift when other children get theirs. Usually, this is a day when all children receive gifts of money and sweets from adults. The message is short and rhythmic.

Notes

1 . The Swahili inscription leaves out the question mark. Although punctuation marks are important in conveying the correct meaning, they are always omitted from *kanga* texts.

CHAPTER SIX

KANGA LANGUAGE AND SWAHILI LITERARY TRADITIONS

Cloth is the carrier of written and oral language in both its content and its literary form. Some 120 of the sayings in the sample (16.4 percent) are well known traditional proverbs. In Swahili these are called *methali,* 'model speech' or *mafumbo* 'closed speech'. The semantic significance of a Swahili proverb is conveyed on the *kanga* that says

Fumbo hufumbiwa mjinga mwerevu hutambua
A proverb baffles an ignorant person; an intelligent person recognizes it

Proverbial *kanga* names lead the wearer, donor, and reader alike to recall Swahili wisdom. Both have internalized the wording of the proverb so that when one person begins a proverb it is quite usual for one of the hearers to complete it. The hearer shows familiarity with what is said and accepts the wisdom of the saying. Thus, the first speaker may say

Mchimba kisima
A person who digs a well

As he pauses, the hearer quickly completes the proverb

huingia mwenyewe
himself falls into it

The proverbial message is a reminder of the philosophical statement that both have heard numerous times before.

In Swahili oratory, proverbs not only reinforce and authenticate traditional wisdom; they also raise social consciousness. They provide moral codes and direction. Both the wearer of the message and its reader reassert the wisdom of the provertb. For example:

Akili ni mali
Wisdom is wealth

Dunia duara
The world is a wheel (i.e. goes round)

Mwenye macho haambiwi tazama
He who has eyes is not asked to look

Mwenzako akinyolewa tia maji kichwa
When your companion is being shaved, put water on your head in readiness

Fahali wawili hawakai zizi moja
Two bulls do not live in the same kraal

Mwana umleavyo ndivyo akuavyo
The way you raise a child is the way that child will grow

Kidole kimoja hakivunji chawa
One finger does not kill a louse

Mramba asali harambi mara moja
He who licks honey does not lick it only once

Ukiona vyaelea vimeundwa
If you see them floating, they are well built

Haraka haraka haina baraka
Hurry, hurry has no blessing

Uchungu wa mwana aujuaye mzazi
One who gives birth knows the pain of child bearing

Mkono mtupu haulambwi
An empty hand is not licked

Haba na haba hujaza kibaba
Little and little fills the measure

Polepole ndiyo mwendo
Slowly, slowly [is] the best way
[More haste less speed]

We recognize a proverb by its parallel structure, by its metaphor and by its rhythm. Whether a phrase or a sentence, it consists of two parts: the beginning of the proverb that is the head of the structure and establishes the situation, and a second part that is its completion, the result. In his article, "Proverbs in an East African setting," T. S. Sengo, a Tanzanian professor of Swahili literature, suggests that "What matters is not just the proverb as a literary statement, but its pertinence to the existing problem at that particular time in space. It is both the physical and psychological enactment that brings about the realization of proverbial usage."[1] The parallel structure in proverbial *kanga* messages conveys a situation and its positive or negative result. It also gives the proverb a poetic style. This is an important linguistic feature that reinforces a concept or a message.

In many cases, the parallel structure is built on an identical number of syllables balancing the two parts. The last syllable of the first part sometimes rhymes with the last syllable of the second part, for example,

Hasira hasara

Ha-si-<u>ra</u>   *ha-sa-<u>ra</u>*

3   3

Akili ni mali

A-ki-<u>li</u>   *ni ma-<u>li</u>*

3   3

Mtoto umleavyo ndivyo akuavyo

Mto-to u-mle-a- <u>vyo</u>   *ndi-vyo a-ku-a <u>vyo</u>*

6   6

The first part may consist of several words:

Ukiona vyaelea vimeundwa

U-ki-o-na +   vya-e-le-a vi-me-u-ndwa

4 +   4   4

Among the 750-*kanga* names in the sample, 341 (45.4 per cent) appear by their structure to be "new proverbs" coined to convey contemporary experiences, feelings and ideas. These "new proverbs" are coined to fit contemporary events and situations. All exhibit the features of traditional proverbs: brevity, elegance of style, balanced sentence structure.

Some resemble proverbs on account of their structure and their play on words. For example:

Chunga chungio   *usinichunge mimi*   *siyo mke mwenziyo*

Watch over the sieve   Do not watch over me   I am not a co-wife to you

In the first part of this message, *Chungio* is a strainer or a sieve. The verb is followed by its noun and together they establish a situation. The same root then appears in the negative form of the verb *chunga* in the second part, i.e. *usinichunge*. But, besides meaning to strain, *chunga* also means 'to herd animals.' Hence the punning message concludes 'I am not your co-wife.' In this instance, the message has a tripartite form, a third part reinforcing the command in the second.

Some "new proverbs" rhyme. For example:

Chokochoko si njema mchague la kusema

Provocation is not good; choose what to say

Cha mumeo chako ringia bahati yako

What belongs to your husband belongs to you

Be proud of your good fortune

Nikiweko sikupendezi na kunikosa huwezi
My presence does not please you, yet you cannot do without me

Muokoa nchi ndio mwananchi
The child of the country (a citizen) is the one who saves the country

Mimi ni komba siijazoweya kuomba
I am a *komba* (a bush baby) I am not used to begging

New proverbs that do not rhyme include:

Kazi mbi si mchezo mwema
A bad job is not a good game

Kupata si werevu na kukosa si ujinga
Getting is not cleverness and lacking is not ignorance

Kitamu huliwa kwa hamu
A sweet thing is eaten with fervor

Si mzizi si hirizi bali moyo umeridhi
It is not because of herbal medicine nor is an amulet, the heart is willing

All these new proverbs express human experience and behavior. But, while they may be classified as aphorisms (short pithy sayings) they are not yet sufficiently well known to be considered proverbs. With time and frequency of usage, they may yet become familiar discourse and carry the weight of truth and wisdom.

   Not only in the form of proverbs do *kangas* play an aesthetic role creating and extending Swahili's literary heritage. Some kanga messages are, for example, lines from classical songs or from well-known poems. Examples include

Nimezama kibahari cha mapenzi
Nimekwama kujiepua siwezi
I have drowned in the sea of love
I am stuck I cannot come out of it

Nampenda mpenzi wangu simwachi
mtasema mtachoka hatoki
I love my beloved. You can talk until you get tired
But I will not leave my beloved

Mazowea yana taabu tabia zikilingana
Friendship is hard when two friends are alike in their behavior

An excellent example of how a song becomes a *kanga* message is provided by the famous Swahili singer,

Siti binti Saad (1880-1950.)[2] A verse from one of her most famous songs runs:

> Sikusudi yangu kuacha watani
> Enye walimwengu mwajua yakini
> Apendalo Mungu haliwezekani

This song translates as:

> It was not my intention to leave my homeland.
> Moreover, you human beings are fully aware of this
> No one can undo what God wishes

The last line of Binti Saad's song is now a *kanga* message:

> Apendalo Mngu haliwezekani
> No one can undo what God wishes

Another *kanga* message derives from an old song beginning

> Raha ya dunia   ni mambo matatu
> The comfort of this world   consists of three things

Listeners who are familiar with the song know what these three things are and the *kanga* message reminds them of their importance:

> Ya kwanza afiya   ya pili ni kitu
> Ya tatu bahati   kupendwa na watu
> The first is health   the second is wealth
> And the third is luck   that makes others like you

More recently, the reverse procedure has occured. Swahili composers have begun to take *kanga* messages as inspiration for their Tarab songs. Tarab is a musical performance in which a singer or a group of singers of Swhaili or Arabic songs is accompanied by musicians playing various musical instruments. They usually perform at weddings and other joyous occasions. Two songs from *kanga* messages that I heard recently at a wedding are:

> Si mzizi si hirizi bali moyo umeridhi
> It is because of neither herbal medicine nor an amulet; the heart is willing

and

> Sichagui sibagui anizikaye simjui
> I don't choose I don't discriminate; I don't know who will bury me

A very large proportion of the sayings from the sample (287 or 38.2 per cent) uses ordinary daily discourse and are neither epigrammatic nor proverbial. For example,

Ingawa tumeachana yaliobaki ni mazoea
Although we are separated (divorced), what is left between us is friendship

Nimempenda kwa mengi
I have loved my beloved for many reasons

Wazazi nipeni radhi
Parents, give me your blessings

Wapendanao vigumu kuwamua [kuwaamua]
It is difficult to separate the two people who are in love

INNOVATIONS

There are those *majina* messages that are already well established; there are those that are becoming so; and there are those that are not yet literary traditions. Change and innovation in the layout and function of *kangas* are largely conditioned by social and political events.

The first change that took place in the late nineteen fifties was from the traditional Arabic script that had been known and used by most of the coastal people for centuries, to the Roman script that European missionaries had introduced in the nineteenth century. Most *kangas* bought and sold in East Africa and Oman today appear with a text written in Roman script but, interestingly enough, one recent *leso* from Oman carries an Arabic message written in Arabic script (Figure 37). This may be transcribed as

Nadiym alqalb asàdniy salaamak
Repenting heart, I am happy with your greetings

The second change was the appearance of *kanga bubu*, the *kanga* that does not speak. Figures 26-28 show examples of *kanga bubu*. The informal explanation given for this change was that immediately after the union of Tanganyika and Zanzibar in 1964, tourists as well as some local Tanzanians began using *kangas* to make long dresses. They did not wish to have writing appear across their garments. More recently, people have begun to complain about unpleasant sayings on modern *kangas*. This, too, has led to an increase of *kanga bubu* on the market.

The impact of the tourist trade is also seen in the way *kangas* are now sold in East Africa. For centuries, *kanga* have been sold in pairs and bought in pairs as their original name *nguo mbili* designates. This is confirmed by an old Swahili proverb:

Wa mbili havai moja
A person who is used to wearing two garments does not wear one

Although the majority of *kangas* sold on the market in East Africa are sold in pairs as *nguo mbili,* two cloths, or *pande mbili* or *doti,* two sides, today, a visitor may buy only one half of the *kanga* cloth. The merchant obliges the customer. In 1987, Jeannette Hanby and David Pygott published a small book called *Kangas: 101 Uses.*[3] This tourist innovation suggested that *kangas* might be used in one hundred and one ways! And, indeed, Western travelers use *kangas* as tablecloths, curtains and slip covers for couches and cushions. For Waswahili *kangas* remain *nguo,* clothes with names.

Another tourist-related innovation is *kangas* with messages in English in place of Swahili. Five *kangas* in the sample, all produced in Kenya, carry messages in English only:

İ love you

Hello, Good morning (See figure 35)

Fom Africa with Love

True love never die (sic)

I ♥ you.

Another *kanga*, also from Kenya, has a bilingual name with an English translation as well as its Swahili message (Figure 36).

Akili ni Mali
Ability is Wealth

Another has mixed the two languages within the one message

Fifty fifty *mimi na wewe*
You and I fifty fifty

Whether this trend will continue and become a new style in *kanga* names only time will tell.

The effect of trade and tourism on *kangas* and their messages is clearly seen in Figure 34. This shows a blouse that a friend bought from a Neiman Marcus store in New Jersey. It is made up of pieces of different *kanga* designs. The names are chopped up and mutilated resulting in the complete destruction of the messages. One can recognize pieces of incomplete texts but the messages are lost. Presumably neither the purchaser nor the wearer is aware of the significance of a *kanga* message and its importance.

A very distinctive innovation was a half *kanga* cloth commissioned for the palace of His Majesty Sultan Qaboos bin Said. These are given out by the Palace as gifts on special occasions. They were produced as a limited edition in Muscat, Oman. This innovative idea has since spread to others who wish to commemorate special occasions. Known as *L-Haaf*, its format is the same as that of a *kanga*, a rectangular cloth of 46 by 68 inches. Its centerpiece may bear a picture of one of Oman's historical forts or a similar cultural motif reflecting Oman's heritage (See Figure 38) or it may show a celebrated Omani landscape. It may bear an artistic composition such as the lake with water lilies at the base of high mountains shown in Figure 39. Its message is written in Arabic script.

Like *kanga*, the *l-Haaf* has four borders and women and girls wear it as a shawl over their dresses. Sometimes dresses are made to match *l-Haaf* in which case the *l-Haaf* is made of a more transparent fabric than the dress. The matching piece of fabric for the dress is of the same design and may or may not have a border and a text. This attractive outfit is referred to as 'Salala's cloth' and is produced both locally and overseas in India. Salala is a town on Oman's south coast, a celebrated resort for visitors from throughout the Arabian Gulf in the hot season. These two pieces cost more than a pair of *kangas*. Figure 40 shows this design and the way in which the outfit is worn.

Despite such innovations, the format of *kangas* in East Africa and Oman has remained essentially unchanged regardless of language, script, or design. The message is as important a feature of the *l-Haaf* as it is of the *kanga*. *Kangas* still come in pairs, each with four borders of the same design and colors, and the majority appear with a *jina,* the name or the message. *Kangas* constantly add to Swahili discourse an important literary genre. While the format is maintained, the written discourse that presents the message changes over time. This is highly desirable in a culture that values speech and words. It is to be anticipated that future *kanga* texts will continue to inspire changes, so raising and furthering the consciousness and insight of those who wear them and those who read them.

Notes

1. T.S. Sengo, "Proverbs in an East African setting" in Werner Graebner (ed.), *Sokomo Popular Culture in East Africa* (Amsterdam, 1992) 67.
2. See Shaaban Robert, *Siti Bint Saad* (Dar es Salaam, 1961).
3. Jeanette Hanby and David Pygott, *Kangas: 101 Uses (* Nairobi, 1987)

CONCLUSION

As we have seen, language contact between Omani Arabic and Swahili initially took place before the first century A.D. when traders from Arabia and Waswahili from Africa sailed along the Azanian Ocean coast in search of commodities. The need for trade goods generated labels in order to itemize them. Thus, for example, a piece of cloth that was worn around the waist was known in East Africa as *unguo*, *upande* or *shuka*. Burton tells us that the coastal Waswahili called it *unguo*, those from interior knew it as *upande*, and the Arabs called it *shukka* (*shuqqah*).

Al-Idris, an Arab historian of the twelfth century reported that people in the towns of the coastal region of the Indian Ocean wore two pieces of cloth, one on top and one below the body and this was established in the fourteenth century by Ibn BaTTuTa. Two centuries later Barbosa, a Portuguese traveler and trader observed the existence of cotton and clothes in East Africa.

In the seventeenth century n*guo* came to signify a better quality of cloth. Perhaps (and we can only speculate) *nguo mbili*, two pieces, was a length of cloth produced on the mainland where cotton was grown. It will be recalled that by the 1820's, Owen was stating that the two pieces of the same materials that Congo princesses were wearing (i.e. a four yard length cut in half) were English manufactured. Presumably the mills of Manchester and Liverpool also used cotton imported from Egypt, India, and North America, as well as East African cotton.

Around 1865, Steere, as well as others, stated that a long piece of cloth of double length was used as a two-piece garment that in Zanzibar and Kenya came to be known as *kisutu*. From the available historical documents, it is clear that by the mid nineteenth century there were many types of cloth in East Africa ranging from cottons to silks and brocades.[1] By the 1900s, the word *kanga* appears and replaces the word *kisutu*. *Kanga* signified the two pieces of cloth that were joined as a pair while *kisutu* came to mean a specific design of *nguo mbil*i worn by a bride after she performs a ritual bath on her wedding day. It is not without significance that the cloth that covers the Ka'ba, the sacred Black Stone in Mecca, is called *al-Kiswatu-lshareefah,* a term related to *kisutu*. The *nguo mbili* of yesteryears is today's *kanga* in Tanzania and *leso* in Kenya and Oman. Hence our search for the garment's evolutionary career from *nguo* to *kanga* is completed.

Waswahili choose a *kanga* not only for its aesthetic design but also for its vocative message and it is bought or given as a gift accordingly. *Kangas* have a social function and their messages carry further than the buyer and the wearer. The majority of the messages are of a social-cultural nature. They represent human relationships, attitudes and values. They talk about feelings, grievances, expectations and interests. Women identify themselves and assert albeit anonymously, their individuality through *kanga* messages.

Today, their main focus seems to be on social interaction and — because of social and economic changes—a mother's role is emphasized. *Majina,* names on *kangas,* stress certain qualities above others. These are patience, tolerance, kindness and getting along with others. They instruct in duties and obligations. They call attention to health over wealth. In short, they express the values and norms that have long been important to the well-being of Swahili society and these are timeless. The reason for these emphases rather than others may be that *kangas* are mostly worn indoors at home and at social gatherings such as weddings and funerals. A familial message is therefore most appropriate and relevant. They are not worn in offices or workplaces where competition might be rife.

Nevertheless *kangas* are also used these days, at political and social gatherings. Their function has expanded beyond that of a form of dress. They are archives of changing events and mark the history of a people. The significance of *kangas* may therefore be seen within an historical and social context. Messages recall past historical events and influence social interaction in the present.

Despite the popularity of the social message, in our changing world the names of *kangas* have recently acquired a new element and play a new role. Out of the 750 *kanga* names in my sample 24 (3.2 percent) carry political meaning or a political implication. This is not a large number compared with those of social relevance, yet it would appear to reflect a trend. These political messages refer to identity and the ideologies with which the society is confronted. The names talk about policies and participation in development. Political awareness affects the message suggesting both the new role of women in society and their involvement in national development. It will be interesting to trace this transformation in the future.

Kangas function as carriers of Swahili oral and written tradition. They carry the past into the present. They represent both the old and the contemporary. They are handed down from generation to generation. They have been in use for centuries. They are an artistic tradition that has survived to reflect today's constant political, social and economic change. *Kangas* are Waswahili archives for their words and the ideas they express provide the researcher with access to the past as well as the ever changing present.

Kanga messages are socially focused and present both women's and men's opinions. They regulate social behavior. To many Waswahili the *jina*, the name, with the message it conveys is the most important feature of the *kanga*. It does not only enhance the aesthetic beauty of the garment, but to them, it represents an event, a behavior, a situation or an experience. Most messages are contemporary. They convey in writing socially expressible and inexpressible feelings. Written on cloth, the messages last longer and are remembered longer. They enunciate, instruct and give direction; they deal with a broad range of messages about human conduct. *Kangas* use words to convey social values and issues and thus are capable of hurting as well as doing well.

Kangas preserve past metaphors of discourse and create new utterances. They have served as a mirror of women's experiences, concerns, participation and outlook on life over several centuries. As these have broadened, so a traditional *kanga* culture has been kept alive and enhanced. Wherever modern Swahili women have traveled, they build cultural links anew. Along with the Swahili language, cuisine and music, *kangas* are agents of cultural continuity across a vast Diaspora. A twelfth-century fashion remains as popular today in Swahili communities as far apart as China, Indonesia, Russia and the United States. *Kanga* names speak to all.

APPENDIX

KANGA TEXTS COLLECTED BETWEEN 1984 - 2001

The 750 texts may be arranged into nine categories:

Friendship, Love and Marriage
Hostility and Resentment
Family Relationships
Wealth and Strength, Cooperation and Competition
Patience, Tolerance and Faith
Experience, Knowledge and Action
Kindness and Generosity
Idd Greetings
Politics and National Identity

A SAMPLE OF SEVEN HUNDRED AND FIFTY KANGA NAMES

FRIENDSHIP, LOVE AND MARRIAGE

1. Mpende akupendae
    Love the one who loves you
2. Pendo letu liwe nono
    May our love be strong
3. Duniyani kuna pepo wawili wapendanapo
    There is Heaven on earth when two people are in love
4. Ghafula yamenisibu
    Suddenly it (love) has affected me
5. Nakufikiri hutoki moyoni nakutamani uje mikononi
    I think of you. You are always in my heart. I long for you to be in my arms
6. Umpendae usimfiche siri
    Do not hide a secret from the one you love
7. Jaraha la moyoni haliponi
    A sore in the heart does not heal./A broken heart doesn't heal
8. Nataraji kukuona kwa sifa yako
    I hope to see you because of your good reputation
9. Si mimi ni moyo
    It is not me. It is my heart [talking]
10. Fanza bidii tuonane
    Do your best so we may see each other
11. Mapenzi ni nusu ya wazimu
    Love is being half-mad

12.   Nikiweko sikupendezi na kunikosa huwezi
      When I am with you you are not pleased with me, yet you cannot live without
      me

13.   Nimezama kibahari cha mapenzi. Nimekwama kujiupua siwezi
      I have drowned in the sea of love. I am stuck I cannot submerge

14.   Ukila zabibu utatoa majibu
      If you eat grapes, you will give out the answer

15.   I love you.   (No Swahili is given)

16.   Heart to heart. Especially for you (No Swahili is given)

17.   Siri ya wawili
      Secret is of two

18.   Si uzuri kutengana
      Separation is not right

19.   Usibadilike
      Do not change

20.   Tusitengane mimi na wewe
      You and I should not part

21.   Akheri Bwana
      Good morning my husband

22.   Mapenzi hayachagui kabila
      Love does not choose a lineage

23.   Nakupenda kama macho yangu
      I love you as I love my eyes

24.   Apendaye chongo huita kengeza
      A person who is in love calls blindness a squint

25.   Usiache mbachao kwa msala upitao
      Do not give up your straw mat for a rug that passes by

26.   Tulia tuishi wazuri haweshi
      Settle down and let us live together; the beautiful ones are not scarce/are not in
      short supply

27.   Tulizana mpenzi hakika mimi ni wako
      Settle down my beloved; I am truly yours

28.   I ngawa tumeachana yaliobaki ni mazoea
      Although we are separated (divorced), what is left between us is friendship

29.   Moyo wa kupenda hauna subira
      A loving heart has no patience

30.   Usinione nasinziya usemayo nasikia
      Do not see me dozing: I hear what you say

31.   Mpende akupendaye asiyekupenda usiwe na haja naye
      Love the one who loves you. Do not care for the one who does not

32.   Mapenzi ni kikohozi hayawezi kufichika
      Love is like a cough; it cannot be hidden

33.   Wagombanao ndio wapatanao
      Those who quarrel are the ones who reconcile

34. Harufu yako yaburudisha moyo wangu
    Your scent (smell) sooths my heart
35. Harufu yako yaniburudisha moyo wangu
    Your scent (smell) cools my heart
36. Raha ya dunia ni mambo matatu
    The comfort of this world consists of three things
37. Ukiona vyaelea vimeundwa
    If you see them floating they are well built
38. Sitakuacha kamwe
    I will never leave you
39. Tuombeane maisha mema
    Let us pray for good life for each other
40. Akupendae humwona kwenye haja
    The one who loves you shows up when you are in need
41. Kama hampendi nampenda mie
    If he/she does not love him/her, I do
42. Usifikirie yaliyopita
    Do not think of the past
43. Tabasamu yako yanifurahisha roho yangu
    Your smile makes me happy
44. Mapenzi ni vitendo sio maneno
    Love is actions not words
45. Kaa nao lakini ujue tabia zao
    Stay with them but know their habits
46. Cheka nao ujue tabia zao
    Laugh with them so that you may know their ways
47. Nakula nae nacheka nae sina hamu nae.
    I eat with him/her, I laugh with him/her, but I do not desire him/her
48. Lila na fila hazitengamani
    May be and actuality are not compatible
49. Tulia kwanza
    First, calm down
50. Mkono kwa mkono
    Hand to hand
51. Aliekando haangukiwi na mti
    He who keeps at a distance, a tree does not fall on him
52. Wawili si mmoja
    Two people are not one
53. Ushikwapo shikamana
    Hold onto the one who holds on you
54. Jaribu kulitunza pendo letu
    Try and care for our love
55. Maneno matamu hulainisha moyo mgumu
    Sweet words soften a hard heart

56.   Kauli njema yashinda tajiri [utajiri]
        Good words are better than wealth

57.   Badili tabia tuanze upya
        Change your habit so we may start anew

58.   Mpenzi wangu ni zahabu [dhahabu] kupenda si ajabu
        My beloved is gold; loving him/her is not a surprise

59.   Cha mumeo chako ringia bahati yako
        What belongs to your husband belongs to you. Be proud of your good luck

60.   Ni zako zabibu zile taratibu
        The grapes are yours eat them slowly

61.   Niache na dhiki yangu nimetulia nyumbani kwangu
        Leave me with my miseries. I am settled in my home

62.   Zawadi ya tunda pokeya usitupe yale mazoweya
        Do receive a gift of a fruit. Do not abandon friendship

63.   Fifty fifty mimi na wewe
        You and I fifty fifty

64.   Ahadi ni deni
        A promise is a debt

65.   Japo umeniacha moyoni hujanitoka
        Although you have left me (divorced me), you are still in my heart

66.   Si mzizi si hirizi bali moyo umeridhi
        It is neither herbal medicine nor amulet; my heart is willing

67.   Wewe ni wangu tu
        You are mine

68.   Usinione nimechoka moyoni nimekuweka
        Do not see that I am tired; I have put you inside my heart

69.   Tupendane mpaka waulizane
        Let us love one anther so they can gossip

70.   Nakuveka pete yangu uwe mchumba wangu
        I am putting a ring on your finger you are my fiancée

71.   Usimpende akakujua hawachi kujizuzua
        Do not love someone to the extent that he/she knows you love him/her lest, he/she be conceited

72   Si mimi moyo wapenda
        It is not me my heart is in love

73.   Dawa ya penzi ni penzi
        The medicine of love is love

74.   Mapenzi yetu yawe daima
        May our love last forever

75.   Powa roho yako mimi wako peke yako
        Calm down your heart I am yours alone

76.   Moto hauzai moto
        A fire does not give birth to a fire

77.   Kipendacho moyo dawa
        What the heart loves is medicine

78. Sumu ya mimi ni wewe
    My poison is you
79. Sichagui sibagui anizikaye simjui
    I do not choose I don't discriminate; I don't know who will bury me
80. Mpenzi nenda salama urudi salama
    Go safely and return safely dearest
81. Usinipende kwa moja nipende kwa yote
    Do not love me for one thing love me for everything
82. Lete raha mpenzi moyo hauna subira
    Dearest give me love my heart cannot wait
83. Mpende ajuaye pendo
    Love the one who understands love
84. Nampenda mpenzi wangu mtasema mtachoka hattoki [hatoki]
    I love my beloved and you will talk until you get tired he/she will not leave me
85. Yaliyonifika si haba sitoacha mahaba
    I have suffered a lot (not a little) but I will not stop loving
86. Sitobadili pendo langu kwa jambo la kusikia
    I will not change my love because of gossip
87. Wewe ndio ufunguo wa moyo wangu
    You are the key to my heart
88. Wawili wakipendana adui hana nafasi
    When two people are in love there is no room for an enemy
89. Huba yako inatunza pendo langu
    Your affection sustains my love
90. Pendo halina haraka hasumbuki mwenye radhi
    There is no haste in love the blessed one does not suffer
91. Huba zako hungarisha maisha yangu
    Your love brightens up my life
92. Sabahu lkheri mpenzi
    Good morning beloved
93. Mahaba wataka nini kwa mimi masikini
    Love, what do you want from me a destitute?
94. Mpendwa hujipendekeza
    The one who is loved makes oneself pleasant
95. Ingawa uko mbali kukukumbuka si achi
    Although you are far away I never stop thinking of you
96. Niko na wewe mpaka mwisho yakiwa
    I am with you until it happens
97. Kiapo nakuapia mwengine hatatokea
    You have my promise there will be nobody else
98. Kipendacho moyo ni dawa
    What the heart loves is medicine
99. Pendo ni tamu kwa mwenye kujua
    Love is sweet to the one who knows how to love

100. Simuhitaji wa dhahabu wala fedha muhitaji wa mapenzi ukiweza
   I am in need of neither gold nor silver; I need love if you are capable of giving it

101. Mapenzi hayawezi kufichika
   Love cannot be hidden

102. Tulia tuishi vizuri
   Settle down and let us live in harmony

103. Raha ya moyo wangu mimi kupendwa na wewe
   My heart is at peace by being loved by you

104. Mimi na wewe pete na kidole
   You and I are like a ring and a finger

105. Sifa ya mke ni kumkirimu mumewe
   The wife is praised when she entertains her husband

106. Mpenzi ni pepe [nipepee]
   Dearest one, would you fan me

107. Haba na haba hutaza [hujaza] mahba. [mahaba]
   Love increases little by little

108. Mapenzi ni mali ya moyo
   Love is the heart's wealth

109. Umpendaye mpe kitu chema
   Give the one you love something nice

110. Apendae hachi hasara
   The one who is in love does not fear loss

111. Mwaniona napenda nyoyo zenu zadunda
   You see me in love and your hearts are beating/disturbed

112. Raha ya mapenzi kupenda
   The fun of love is loving

113. Haba na haba hujaza mahaba
   Love increases little by little

114.. Nakupenda kwa dhati
   I love you sincerely

115. Powa roho yako mimi ni wako
   Calm down your heart I am yours

116. Raha ya mapenzi kupendana
   The fun/bliss of love is to love one another

117. Macho yameona moyo umechagua
   The eyes have seen and the heart has chosen

118. Kitamu huliwa kwa hamu
   A sweet thing is eaten with fervor

119. Asmini nimetandika kitandani mimi wako wewe sijui wa nani
   I have spread jasmine on the bed I am yours but I don't know to whom you belong

120. Nampenda anipendae asonipenda sina hajane [haja naye]
   I love the one who loves me. I do not need the one who doesn't

121. Kama hanipendi nampenda mie
   If he/she does not love me I love him/her

122. Nipende kwa nia nipate kutulia
Love me truly, so I may settle down
123. Qais and Layla
Romeo and Juliet. (Two lovers in Arabic folklore)
124. Tabia zikiwa ndizo daima sina mizozo
When behavior is right I never have problems
125. Pendo ni nuru
Love is light
126. Tuugane [Tuungane] daima kwa upendo
Let us always unite in love
127. Mapenzi hayana dawa
There is no cure (medicine) for love
128. Ndoa ni fungo la heri
Marriage is a good (blessed) unity
129. Tuishi milele kwa furaha
May we live together happily everafter
130. Maneno yako asali yanene unaposwali
Your words are as sweet as honey utter them in your prayers
131. Nitakuenzi kama macho yangu
I will treasure you as I treasure my eyes
132. Mola tujalie tuishi daima
Lord, let us always be together
133. Akipenda chongo huita kengeza
He who loves calls one-eyed a squint./Love is blind
134. Uso mzuri hauhitaji urembo
A beautiful face does not require make up (Beautification)
135. Kupendana ni wajibu yataka taratibu
Loving one another is a duty and needs attention
136. Japo masikini nitaishi naye
Even if s/he is poor I will live with him/her
137. Tuishi kwa usalama tuepuke uhasama
Let us live in harmony and avoid hostility
138. Japokuwa mbaya lakini ni wako
Although (I am) ugly (I am/is) yours
139. Dunia ina pepo wawili wapendanapo
There is heaven on earth when two people are in love
140. Ua la chanua mapenzi hutanua
The flower blooms, love glows/expands
141. Wapendanao hupamba tabia zao
Those in love attract one another through their behavior
142. Tuishi kwa wema tupate neema
Let us live together amicably and we may be blessed
143. Habibi wewe ni nuru ya macho yangu
My darling you are the light of my eyes

144.   Nivike pete nicheke wanunao wanune
    Place a ring on my finger and I will be happy and those who sulk will sulk/brood

145.   Bila wewe sikiwezi [sijiwezi] kwa mapenzi sikiwezi [sikuwezi]
    I cannot do without you (and) you are better than I am in affection

146.   Nitazidi kukupenda watu wazidi kusema
    I will love you more so that people may talk (gossip) more

147.   Bora nikose mapenzi kudharauliwa siwezi
    I would rather lose your love than be despised

148.   Karibuni waungwana na harusi ya mwana
    Welcome noble people I have my daughter's/son's wedding

149.   Sitaki lulu wala fedha nataka mapenzi ukiweza
    I want neither pearls nor silver I want love if you are able (to give it to me)

150.   Rafiki mwema ni akikusaidia/akusaidiae kwa dhiki
    A good friend is the one who helps you while you are in need

151.   Mapenzi ni maua
    Love is like flowers

152.   Mimi na wewe kuzama kuzuka
    You and I are together sink or swim

153.   Moyo ni jaraha nipende nione raha
    The heart is a sore love me that I may feel comfortable

154.   Kilicho nivutia ni yako tabia
    What attracted me is your behavior

155.   Pendo ni jeraha nipende nione raha
    Love is a wound; love me so I may feel comfortable

156.   Namshukuru manani kunipatia mwendani
    I thank my Lord for giving me a friend

157.   Karibu karibu wangu muhibu
    Welcome, welcome my dearest

158.   Tupendane kwa dhati tusipotezeane wakati
    Let us love one another sincerely and not waste each other's time

159.   Sina mwingine ila wewe
    I do not have another one but you

160.   Sijachoka bado nakupenda sana
    I am not tired. I still love you very much

161.   Harusi ni nguo ya kheri
    A wedding is a blessed garment

162.   Raha ya nyumba ni masikilizano
    The comfort of the home is getting along with one another

163.   Mwenye pupa hadiriki kula tamu
    A hasty person does not have the time to eat a ripe fruit

164.   Ukae ukijua mapenzi yataniua
    Know that love will kill me

165.   Taka kikutakacho kisichokutaka usiwe na haja nacho
    Want the one who wants you; do not want the one who doesn't

166. Nakuridhia kwa kila hali jua nakupenda kweli
     I satisfy all your needs. You should know that I truly love you
167. Napenda kukuona mpenzi wangu nifuraha ya moyo wangu
     I like seeing you my dear. It is the joy of my heart
168. Apendae hajali
     The one who is in love does not mind (Love is blind)
169. Mapenzi ni gilass yakivunjika/ikivunjika huwa basi
     Love is a glass when it breaks it is gone
170. Pendo letu lenye maana wenyewe tunalithamini
     Our love is real; we value it
171. Ukipenda boga upende na uwa lake
     When you like a pumpkin, you should also like its flower
172. Mwenye kupenda hachoki kuvumilia
     He who is in love is never tired of endurance
173. Furaha ya harusi   Wedding happiness
174. Haina jina
     It does not have a name
175. Kilichohifadhiwa huthaminiwa
     A protected thing is valued
176. Mapenzi yangu zawadi yako
     Your gift is my love
177. Binadamu tupendane mazuri tutendeane
     As human beings, we should love one another and do good for each other
178. Sichagui sibagui anizikaye simjui
     I do not choose I don't discriminate. I don't know who will burry me
179. Anayependa kikweli hachoki kuvumilia
     He who is deeply in love is never intolerant
180. Mapenzi ni majani popote huota
     Love is like grass. It grows anywhere
181. Nakhiari niumie lakini nikuridhie
     I would rather get hurt to please you
182. Mapenzi ni idhilali humdhili apendae
     Love is humiliation. It humiliates he who loves
183. Moyo hausemezeki kwa kitu kipendacho
     The heart cannot be advised against what it loves
184. Pendo lako nalitaka nipate kufurahika
     I want your love so I can be happy
185. Pendo langu mwisho kwake simpi mtu
     My love is only for him/her. I will give it to no one else
186. Mapenzi yako asali ladha isomalizika
     Your love is honey; a taste that does not finish
187. Mahaba ni asali usiongeze sukari
     Love is honey. Don't add sugar
188. Pokea zawadi tuzo [tunzo] lako mpenzi
     My dear, receive a gift as a reward

189.   From Africa with love
190.   No one but you
191.   Mapenzi ni mali ya moyo
        Love is the wealth to the heart
192.   Mapenzi ni gilasi ikivunjika basi
        Love is like a glass. When it breaks it has vanished
193.   Wapendanao ni vigumu kuwamua [kuwaamua]
        It is difficult to separate those who are in love

HOSTILITY AND RESENTMENT

1.   Mchimba kisima huingia mwenyewe
        He who digs a well himself falls into it
2.   Wache waseme
        Let them gossip
3.   Bora kujikwaa dole kuliko ulimi./Heri kujikwaa kidole kuliko ulimi
        It is better to trip/stumble with your toe than with your tongue
4.   Usiniseme
        Don't gossip about me
5.   Maneno yawe mafupi vitendo virefu
        Let the words be short and the actions long
6.   Simba mwenda kimya ndio mla nyama
        The quiet lion eats the meat
7.   Tizama lako
        Mind your own business
8.   Mso hili ana lile
        He who does not have this one has that
9.   Kijicho cha chura hakimzui ng'ombe kunywa maji
        The tiny eyes of the frog do not deter the cow from drinking water
10.   Mwenye nguvu mpishe
        Let the strong one pass
11.   Adui mpende
        Love thy enemy
12.   Mpanda hila huvuna majuto
        One who plants tricks harvests regrets
13.   Mbona husemi nami
        Why don't you talk to me?
14.   Nazi mbovu harabu ya nzima
        A bad coconut spoils the good ones
15.   Wape wape vidonge vyao wakimeza wakitema shauri yao
        Give them; give them their pills (medicine). It is up to them whether they swallow them or spit them. (A verse from a popular song)
16.   Mzaha mzaha hutumbuka usaha
        Too much joking results in an oozing sore

17. Machoni rafiki moyoni mnafiki
    In front of you he is a friend in his heart is a hypocrite
18. Ukistaajabu ya Musa utaona ya Firauni
    If you are surprised by the behavior of Moses, you will see the doings of the Pharaoh
19. Mimi na wangu na wewe na wako chuki ya nini
    I have mine (person) and you have yours; why is there resentment?
20. Ukichukua kwa pupa dunia itakutupa
    If you grab hastily, the world will cast you off
21. Naogopa simba na meno yake siogopi mtu kwa maneno yake
    I am afraid of a lion with his teeth. I am not afraid of a person by his words
22. Chanuo baya pale unapochoma
    The comb is bad when you prick yourself
23. Naona ni shoga yangu kumbe ni mkwe mwenzangu
    I see you as my girl friend but you turn out to be my co-wife
24. Mcheka kilema humpata yeye
    He who laughs at a disability gets it
25. Umechezea tufali limekutoa kiburi
    You have played with a brick. It has snatched you of your arrogance
26. Nilikudhani dhahabu kumbe adhabu
    I considered you gold but you are a problem
27. Hasidi mpe kiti akae
    Give an envious person a chair to sit on
28. Utamaliza visigino kwa safari za umbea
    You will wear out the heels of your shoes in tale bearing
29. Ulijuwaje. Kama si umbea
    How did you know, if it were not for prying?
30. Bembea langu limewaudhi walimwengu
    My swing (move) annoys the people
31. Nilijua kiroho kitawauma
    I knew that they would be hurt. (Their souls will be sore)
32. Cheka nao lakini si wema kwako
    Laugh with them but they are not good to you
33. Usimfadhili asiye na haya
    Do not be kind to a shameless person
34. Fitina na pelelezi ni sumu ya mapenzi
    Discord and prying are the poison of love
35. Usinifate
    Don't follow me
36. Jirani mbaya usimwonee haya
    Don't feel shy of a bad neighbor
37. Maji yakimwagika hayazoleki
    When the water is spilt out, it cannot be picked up (No good crying over spilt milk)

38. Mbishi hakosi jibu
    An argumentative person is never without an answer
39. Usimdharau usiyemjua
    Don't despise the one you don't know
40. Shingo huvaa vyombo roho huvaa mambo
    The neck wears jewelry; the soul wears problems
41. Mdomo wako ndo sumu yako
    Your mouth is your poison
42. Ya nini wivu mstahmilivu hula mbivu
    Why are you jealous? A patient person eats what is ripe
43. Chakubimbi ukimwona muogope
    You should be afraid of a rumor-monger when you meet one
44. Chakubimbi mamako
    The rumor-monger is your mother
45. Uongo wa mwenye nyumba si ukweli wa mpangaji
    The lie of the owner of the house is not the same as the truth of the tenant
46. Najutia kinywa changu kumeza kitu kichungu
    I regret my mouth swallowing something bitter
47. Dawa ya homa ni quinine dawa ya ubaya ni nini
    The medicine for a fever is quinine. What is the medicine for evilness
48. Mzigo kichwani kwapa watokeani jasho
    The load is on your head; why does you armpit perspire?
49. Asiyejua maana haambiwi maana
    He who does not know the meaning is not told the significance
50. Ashibaye hamjui mwenye njaa
    A satiated person does not know/recognize the hungry one
51. Neno limesemwa ndani limefikaje hadharani
    The word has been said inside (privately); how has it reached the public?
52. Usinione nimetulia jueni nimeridhika
    Do not see that I have settled down; you should know that I am amenable
53. Wakeleketwao shauri yao
    Those who are annoyed it is up to them/their own business
54. Fitina ni hasidi
    An antagonist is spiteful
55. Kakupa pole fisadi
    The evil one sands you his sympathy
56. Chuki nichukieni roho yangu niachieni
    Hate me but do not deprive me of my soul (addresses more than one)
57. Mlidhani nitakumbuka lakini Mola kanikumbuka
    You thought that I would not forget, but God has remembered me
58. Pole hasidi kwangu hupati kitu
    Sorry, the envious one. You will get nothing from me
59. Sijasema mwanisema jee nikisema
    I have said nothing and you gossip about me. What will happen when I do?

60. Lo Mwenzangu Mbona shingo
    Oh, my friend, what is wrong with your neck (you look sad)?

61. Si mimi ni wewe
    It is not me; it is you

61. Mimi pera kila nifanyalo watu lawakera
    I am a guava. Whatever I do, annoys people

62. Hunilishi hunivishi wala hunibabaishi
    You do not feed me nor clothe me and you will not confuse me

63. Mtammezea mate hamumpati
    You will long for him/her (swallow your saliva), but you will not get him/her

64. Tenda wema mara mia adui akijua umeumia
    Do well a hundred times, but when the enemy knows of it you will be hurt

65. Nenda utakako siwezi vituko vyako
    Go wherever you wish. I cannot tolerate your terrible dealings/behavior

66. Chuki nichukie moyo wangu niachie (Addresses one)
    Hate me but leave alone my heart

67. Mja wa stara nimesitirika muliyo yataka hayajanifika
    As one who merits protection, I am protected. What you wished for me has not happened

68. Fitina mbaya
    A menace is bad

69. Hisani huna na fadhila hukumbuki
    You are not kind and you ungreatful

70. Ni bure zenu fitina tawi haliwi shina
    Your discord is a waste of time. A brunch cannot be a trunk

71. Nimedhani mwenzangu kumbe mke mwenzangu
    I thought that you are my friend, but you are my co-wife

72. Asubuhi na mapema wameshaanza kusema
    They have already started talking (gossiping) this early in the morning

73. Mola tunusuru midomo ya waja isitudhuru
    God protect us from peoples' mouths

74. Huba huna na hisani hukumbuki.
    You have no love and you do not remember kindness

75. Kiburi si maungwana
    Conceit is not honorable

76. Paka wa jirani usimkaribishe ndani
    Do not let in (welcome) a neighbor's cat

77. Utamaliza gesi kwa kupika/kupikia mfupa
    You will finish the gas by cooking a born

78. Ala. Kumbe
    So it is so!

79. Usitaratambe huna lako jambo
    Do not brag; you are worthless

80. Moyo umejaa nyongo kwa maneno ya uwongo
    The heart is full of bile because of lies

81. Mambo yangu yameshamchangua
     My doings have mastered him/her
82. Kasuku toa ushahidi watu waridhike
     Parrot, give the evidence so the people will be satisfied
83. Ziko shamba zakuasha
     They (hot chillies) are at shamba and are itching/burning you
84. Asiyeweza kuniumba kuniumbua hawezi
     He that cannot create me cannot disfigure me
85. Lia na tabia yako usilaumu wenzako
     Cry because of your habit; do not blame your companions
86. Mimi maji wewe moto nakuzima
     I am the water and you are the fire I extinguish you
87. Paka shume mtaani kwenu halahala vitoweo vyenu
     A tom cat is in your neighborhood; watch out over your meats [wives or children]
88. Punguza kutembea tuishi nyumbani
     Go out less, so we may stay at home
89. Mimi kawaida yangu sijui wewe limbukeni
     This is ordinary to me, but I do not know what it is to you the novice
90. Sisemi Me! Sisemi mie
     I do not say ME (English "me" or goat's bleating me) I do not say I
91. Hata ukinichukia ukweli nitakwambia
     Even if you dislike me, I will tell you the truth
92. Siri yako usimwambie jirani
     Do not tell a neighbor your secret
93. Kila siku ugomvi tutapatana lini
     We are fighting daily. When will we reconcile?
94. Hata ukifanya makeke kila mtu na bahati yake
     Even if you cause trouble, each person has his luck
95. Mambo yangu yamefana mtabaki mkifinyana
     I have succeeded while you will keep on pinching one another
96. Kaa chini ujiulize ukipata jibu nieleze
     Sit down and ask yourself, and when you get an answer let me know
97. Sijasema mwanisema je nikisema
     I have said nothing and you are gossiping about me. What will happen when I do?
98. Mwenyewe nimeingia bomba mtashikilia
     I have joined willingly you are spreading wrong information
99. Palipo riziki hapakosi mnafiki
     Where there is wealth there is a hypocrite
100. Ukiwa tapeli maisha yako yatafeli
     If you are a conman, your life will fail
101. Sitokula jikoni kwa kuogopa jirani
     I will not eat in the kitchen for fear of the neighbor

102. Wananiona mashangingi wakerekao na wakereke mimi sitoki kwake
The envious ones are looking at me. Let those who are upset be upset. I am not leaving him/her

103. Kishindo cha mashua haishindi (hakishindi) bahari
The gust of the boat does not defeat the sea

104. Mmesahau kazi zenu kutwa kunisengenya
You have forgotten (ignored) your work while you are all day scandalizing me

105. Wameshindwa wenye meno utayaweza wewe kibogoyo
Those with teeth could not succeed let alone you who is toothless

106. We! Kinyau nyau kikiya cha pweza
You. A little kitten and a small tail of an octopus

107. Sitokula gizani kwa kumuogopa jirani
I will not eat in the dark for fear of a neighbor

108. Chunga chungio usinichunge mimi siyo mke mwenziyo
Watch over the sieve (strainer). Do not watch over (strain) me, I am not a co-wife to you

109. Ninaishi kidaktari msemayo natafakari mwisho natowa vidonge vikali
I live like a doctor. I consider what you say, and then I prescribe strong pills

110. Muwongo mpe chai kwa bakuli aelezee vizuri
Give a liar tea in a large bowl so he may provide details

111. Penye riziki hapakosi fitina. Usijaze masusu kwa mambo yasokuhusu
Where there is sustenance (prosperity) there is discord. Do not fill up baskets with things that do not concern you

112. Pita ukiringa usijali wajinga
Walk proudly; do not pay attention to the ignorants

113. Hata mkiniwekea vigengi bado
Even if you gang against me, I will not stop

114. Mwenye wivu hali akashiba
A jealous person does not eat to his heart content/does not satisfy his hunger

115. Japo kuwa mjanja kwangu mimi ni mteja
Although you are shrewd, to me you are a merely a novice/a client

116. Mimi ni shina sishituki na matawi
I am the base (the foundation) I am not startled by the branches

117. Nilijua roho zitawauma
I knew they would be upset

118. Hata mkinichukia riziki hamtonifungia
Even if you hate me, you cannot stop my sustenance

119. Hasidi awe na meno meupe roho yake nyeusi
Even though an envious person may have white teeth his heart is black

120. Yakinikifu nitayajibu bila ya aibu
If they suit me, I will respond without shame

121. Mama mkwe ni jipu la utosi
A mother-in- law is an abscess in the middle of the head

122. Kama wewe moshi mimi moto
If you are the smoke, I am the fire

123. Nimependwa na kaka yako wifi tulia
      Sister in law cool down, your brother loves me

123. Sishituki na mapambo hata ukiwa mrembo
      Even if you are of style, your ornaments do not astound me

124. Ingawa sina lakini siadhiriki
      Even though I don't have (am poor), I am not debased

125. Hata mkinuna la kunifanya hamuna
      Even if you sulk, there is nothing you can do to me

126. Fumbo mfumbie mjinga kwangu umetoka kappa
      Cast your riddle to an ignoramus; to me you will be the looser

127. Baya mlonitakia silo Mungu aliloni jaaliya
      The bad thing that you have wished for me is not what God has bestowed on
      me

128. Kunyamaza si kushindwa
      Silence does not mean defeat

129. Shoga mdokozi usimwachie mdomo wazi
      Do not leave your mouth open to a friend who grabs

130. Yenu du ya wenzenu midomo juu
      Your mouths are shut when it concerns you, but you talk when it is about others

131. Sitawajibu kamwe watanyamaza wenyewe
      I will never answer them; they will stop on their own

132. Watasema mchana usiku watalala
      They wil talk/gossip in the daytime, but they will sleep at night

133. Chuki nichukie moyo wangu uniachie
      Hate me, but leave my heart alone

134. Kila leo ugomvi tutapatana lini
      We quarrel daily; when will we reconcile?

135. Punguza umbea uishi vizuri mtaani
      Be less nosy so you may live in harmony in the neighborhood

136. Hakika nimesadiki paka hana urafiki
      Indeed, I now believe that a cat is not a friend

137. Niliyajua hayo siku nyingi sana
      I knew that many days ago

138. Sitalipiza lakini sitasahau
      I will not revenge nor will I forget

139. Bora lawama kuliko fedheha
      Blame is better than disgrace

140. Mlidhani/Ulifikiri nitaoza nimepata wa kunipoza
      You (plural /singular) thought I would rot; I have found someone to console me

141. Shanuo baya pale linapokuchoma
      A shanuo (a pick/a type of a comb) becomes bad when it pricks you

142. Ukali wa jicho washinda wembe
      An eye is sharper than a razor blade

143. Halahala mti na macho
      Be careful of a stick touching your eyes

144. Heri udongo ukufukie kuliko binaadamu akuchukie
     You are better off dead and buried under the soil than being hated by a human being

145. Mbaazi ukikosa mauwa husingizia jua
     When a pigeon pea plant does not bloom, it blames the sun

146. Si kila mwenye makucha huwa simba
     Not every clawed animal is a lion

147. Maneno makali hayavunji mfupa
     Sharp words do not break a bone

148. Bure mnajisumbua
     You are troubling yourselves for nothing

149. Likinifika nitakujibu
     I will answer you when I receive your message

150. Nia safi hairogwi
     Good intention is not bewitched

151. Kutesana kwa zamu
     He who tortures another gets tortured in return

152. Umezoea uhasama kwangu mimi hupati kitu
     You are used to hostility but from me you will get nothing

153. Sikwambii neno jicho linakutosha
     I will not say anything to you. My eye looking at you is enough

154. Zimalize zako ari sishituki moyo wangu
     Exert yourself (exhaust your pride). My heart is not startled

155. Usijifanye machachari kumbe mtangazaji habari
     Do not be restless; so you are a news monger

156. Yalonifika si haba sitoacha mahaba
     Although I have gone through a lot, I will not give up love

157. Mimi ni mpera kila nifanyalo lawakera
     I am a guava tree whatever I do irritates them

158. Fumbo mfumbie mjinga mwerevu hutambua
     Cast your riddle to an ignorant person. An intelligent one recognizes it

159. Ulimi ni panga
     The tongue is a sword

160. Majuto ni mjukuu huja kinyume
     Regret is like a grand child it comes after the action

161. Bahati huenda kwa wabaya wazuri wakalia ngowa
     Luck goes to those who are ugly and the beautiful ones are jealous

162. Mnyonge kuteseka mchawi kwake furaha
     When the weak one suffers the exorcist is happy

163. Wivu sina sitaki shirika
     I am not jealous, but I do not want sharing

164. Wapende wao wakipenda wenzao huwa mwao
     It is all right for them to fall in love. When others do, it is disapproved (it is a big thing)

FAMILY RELATIONSHIPS

1. Uchungu wa mwana aujuaye mzazi
   The one who gives birth knows the pain of child bearing
2. Mama hana kijicho
   A mother does not envy her child. (is not jealous)
3. Mzaa chema
   One who gives birth to what is good
4. Nani kama mama
   Who is like the mother?
5. Mama awe chambo cha haki duniani
   Let your mother be the source of justice in your world
6. Mla nawe hafi nawe ila mzaliwa nawe
   He who eats with you does not die with you unless he is born with you
7. Mke wa nyumbani mwangaza wa chumbani
   A wife from home is light in the room
8. Sifa ya mume kupamba mke
   A man's reputation is from the way he adorns his wife
9. Mcheza kwao hutunzwa
   He who dances at home is rewarded
10. Watoto laleni niseme na bwana
    Children go to sleep so I may talk to my husband
11. Hakuna kama mama
    There is no one like the mother
12. Jicho la mama ni kama bunduki
    The mother's eye is like a gun
13. Ndugu wawili wakipigana chukua jembe ukalime na wakipatana chukua ukavune
    When two siblings fight, take your plough and go and farm; when they reconcile go and harvest
14. Radhi ya mama ni hatari ya mwana
    It is dangerous for the child when the mother withholds her blessings
15. Mama ni mama japo kuwa ni rikwama./hata akiwa rikwama
    The mother is the mother even if she were a rackety lorry/van
16. Mama nipe radhi kuishi na watu kazi
    Mother, give me your blessings because living with other people is hard work
17. Ulomlia mayai kumtoa ni taabu
    The one for whom you have eaten eggs, aborting it is difficult
18. Mume mwenye mama huna mamlaka naye
    You have no control over a husband who has a mother
19. Kifo cha jamaa arusi
    Dying with others is like being in a wedding
20. Kulea mimba si kazi; kazi kulea mwana
    To care for pregnancy is not hard work but raising the child is hard work
21. Nimechoka kulinda mlango mtoto kanishinda kwa mipango
    I am tired of keeping an eye on the door, the child defeats me with her strategies

22. Dua lako mama siku ya leo ni rehema
    Mother, your prayer today (in these days) brings God's compassion
23. Ng'ombe haelemewi na nunduye
    The cow is not burdened by its hump
24. Kitu gani kimshindacho mama
    What thing defeats the mother?
25. Maziwa ya mama ni bora
    Mother's milk is best
26. Radhi ya mama ni bora
    Mother's blessing is best
27. Mwana msikizi haambiwi mara mbili
    An attentive child is not told something twice
28. Radhi ya mama yashinda mali ya dunia
    Mother's blessing is better than any worldly wealth
29. Mcha mwana kulia hulia yeye
    He who is afraid of the child's crying will end up crying
30. Mwana umleavyo ndivyo akuavyo
    The way you raise the child is the way he will grow
31. Wazazi walio wema wajua manufaa ya watoto
    Good parents know what is good for children
32. Mama yangu mpenzi kumkosa siwezi
    I cannot do without her my dearest mother
33. Mimi nimekiri mapenzi ya wazee wawili
    I have acknowledged the love of two parents
34. Ukifurahisha wazazi utapata radhi
    If you please your parents, you will be blessed
35. Neema ya wazee furaha ya watoto
    Parents' prosperity is their children's joy
36. Shika ya wazazi upate radhi
    Hold on to what your parents say and you will be blessed
37. Mke mwema pambo la nyumba
    A good wife adorns the home
38. Mtaka cha mvunguni huinama
    He who wants to get something from under the bed must stoop for it
39. Udugu ni kufaana udugu si kufanana
    Brotherhood is being helful to one another. Brothers do not have to resemble
    one another
40. Ukifurahisha wazazi utapata radhi
    If you please your parents, you will get their blessings
41. Radhi ya mama ni sitara ya mwana
    Mother's blessing is the child's protection
42. Hakuna mlezi ashindae mama
    No foster parent takes the place of the mother
43. Mama mlezi kanileya kwa mapenzi
    My foster mother raised me with affection

44. Radhi ina manufaa
     Blessing (of the parents) is beneficial
45. Hakuna mpenzi kama mzazi wako
     No one loves you more than your parent
46. Upendo huleta amani nyumbani
     Love brings peace in the home
47. Roho ya mzazi haikosi wasiwasi
     A parent's heart is never without worries
48. Radhi ya mama ni utajiri wa haki mbele ya molla
     The mother's blessing is the rightful wealth in front of the Lord
49. Dua lako mama siku ya leo ni rehema
     Mother, your prayer today (in these days)is a blessing
50. Mama sina cha kukulipa zaidi ya shukurani
     Mother I have nothing more to repay you with than my gratitude
51. Nikulipe nini mama
     Mother, what can I repay you?
52. Pokea hidia [hidaya] ya Iddi mama
     Mother, accept Idd present
53. Mama mlezi nakupenda kama macho yangu
     My foster mother (who has raised me), I love you as I love my eyes
54. Waja umbukeni mimi na mama yangu tunadunda
     Folks you should be ashamed of yourselves. My mother and I are geting
     along well
55. Japo mama kakuzaa na mlezi usimdharau
      Although your mother has given birth to you, do not ignore your foster
     mother
56. Nikupe zawadi gani mama
     My mother, what present should I give you?
57. Nimetembea kila pembe namtafuta nani kama mama
     I have searched in every corner looking for someone who is like my mother
58. Radhi ya mama ni neema
     Mother's blessing is a comfort
59. Nimpe zawadi gani mama
     What present should I give my mother?
60. Upendo huleta baraka nyumbani
     Love brings blessings to the home
61. Wazazi nawaenzi nipate radhi
     Toget their blessings I respect my parents
62. Sifa ni ya mama mlezi
     The compliments are to the mother who raised the child
63. Kicheko cha mtoto ni furaha kwa wazazi
     The child's laughter is the parents' happiness
64. Mungu nipe mwema kama mama yangu
     God give me someone as good as my mother

65. Mke ni kiungo cha familia
   A wife is a family's linkage/A wife bonds a family
66. Tai ya bwana
   My husband's bow tie
67. Asiyesikia la mkuu huvunjika guu
   He who does not listen to his elder's word will break his leg
68. Udongo uwahi ulimaji
   Mould the clay while it is still damp
69. Eid Mubarak mapenzi yangu na wewe ni maisha yetu
   Idd Greetings. Our love is forever
70. Mtoto akimnyenyekea mama hakosi fungu lake
   When a child respects his mother, he gets his share
71. Radhi ya mama ni bora kuliko mali
   The mother's blessing is better than wealth
72. Pokea mama zawadi japo hailingani na malezi
   My mother, receive a gift even though it does not match my upbringing
73. Hongera wazazi pongezi kwa mlezi
   Congratulations to the parents and bravo to the foster parent
74. Mke wa awali ni wewe aziza
   My first wife is you the dearest one
75. Pepo yako chini ya miguu ya mama yako
   Your heaven lies at your mother's feet
76. Muenzi enzi kama kiyoo mume nouguyo [nduguyo]
   The husband is your brother (cousin) you should take care of him as you take
   care of a delicate piece of glass
77. Hakuna mwana asiye na mama
   There is no child who does not have a mother
78. Mama nambari wani hana mpinzani
   My mother is number one (the closest person to me); no one can compete with
   her
79. Malezi mema muongozo wa dunia
   Good upringing/nurturing is guidance in this world
80. Usisahau wazazi.
   Don't forget your parents
81. Mke hapigwi kwa fimbo hupigwa kwa maneno
   A wife is not to be hit with a cane but is punished with words
82. Nakula naye nalala naye lakini sina hamu naye
   I eat with him/her and I sleep with him/her but I do not desire him/her
83. Nasema naye nacheka naye moyoni sina hamu naye
   I speak to him/her and I laugh with him/her but in my heart, I do not desire him/
   her
84. Mama ni kasha langu umebeba uzito wangu
   Mother, you are my suitcase; you have carried my weight
85. Moyo unafurahika mama akiona mtoto kastirika
   A mother is happy when she sees her child well protected

86. Mola nipe wema kama mama yangu
    God, make me as good as my mother
87. Usinikere darling namlaza mtoto naja
    Don't bother me darling. I will come when I have put the child to sleep
88. Hongera mwanangu
    Congratulation, my child
89. Idumu ndoa yetu tulojaaliwa na Mungu
    May the marriage that God has bestowed on us last
90. Harusi ni tamu sote tuwe na hamu
    A wedding is sweet (joyful) and we should all look forward to it
91. Mke mwema ni ua nyumbani huchanua
    A good wife is a flower which blooms in the home
92. Ashante [Ahsante] mama ni wewe
    Thank you. You are my mother
93. Ukipata cheo usisahau mkeo
    Do not forget your wife when you get your promortion

WEALTH AND STRENGTH, COOPERATION AND COMPETITION

1. Nyuki mkali kwa asali yake
   A bee is fiercely protective of its honey
2. Fuata nyuki ule asali
   Follow bees and you may eat honey
3. Niliyotamani nishapata
   I have got what I desired
4. Kingi cha kungojea si kidogo cha kupokea
   The little in hand is better than that for which you have to wait
5. Riziki ni popote
   Sustenance is anywhere
6. Bora ni afya si mali
   Health is better than wealth
7. Maji roho
   Water is soul
8. Usitake ushindani huniwezi asilani
   Do not compete with me you will not win
9. Aso hili ana lile
   He who does not have this thing has the other
10. Kuelekeza si kufuma
    Aiming is not hitting
11. Kupata si uerevu na kukosa si ujinga
    Getting is not being clever and loosing is not being ignorant
12. Mtaka yote hukosa yote
    He who wants all loses all

13. Mvuvi anajua pweza alipo
    The fisherman knows where to find the cuttle-fish
14. Asiyekujua hakuthamini
    He who does not know you does not value you
15. Njaa mwanamalegeza shibe mwana malevya
    Hunger weakens a person but satiation intoxicates him
16. Pesa huzaa pesa
    Money produces money
17. Bahati ni mali
    Luck is wealth
18. Usisafirie nyota ya mwenzio
    Do not be guided by someone elses's star. Follow your own star
19. Mtumai cha nduguye hufa hali masikini
    He who relies on his sibling's wealth dies poor
20. Dau la mnyonge halendi joshi
    A poor man's boat does not sail ahead /sail smoothly
21. Mkono mmoja hauchinji ng'ombe
    One hand does not slaughter a cow
22. Mla mla leo mla jana kala nini
    Today's eater is the winner. What did yesterday's eat?
23. Moyo wangu sultani cha mtu sikitamani
    I have a Sultan's heart. I do not long for someone else's property
24. Tengeneza chako usahau cha mwenzako
    Fix what belongs to you and forget someone else's
25. Ufukara si kilema
    Poverty is not disability
26. Ingawa masikini moyo wangu tajiri
    Although I am poor, my heart is rich
27. Hohe hahe ana siku yake
    A poor man has his good day
28. Usimwingilie aliyepewa kapewa
    He who has been given has been given. Do not interfere with him/ He who has
    has
29. Nala yangu riziki siwajali wanafiki
    I eat what God has given me. I do not pay attention to the hypocrites
30. Kaamil alawsaaf 'atinii diinaar
    The most just one give me a dinaar
31. Lianziapo ndipo liishiapo
    It ends where it begins
32. Hakuna lisilokuwa na mwisho
    There is nothing without an end
33. Bora umaskini wangu kuliko utajiri wako
    My poverty is better than your wealth
34. Si mizizi ni bahati yangu
    It is not the magic of the medicinal root. It is my luck

35. Kibaya changu si chema cha mwenzangu
    An ugly thing that is mine is better than the beautiful thing of another
36. Mja duniani huteswa na chake
    In this world, a person suffers because of what he owns
37. Taa inawaka mbona sikuoni
    The light is on; why are you invisible?
38. Popote nilipo na raha
    I am comfortable where ever I am
39. Usidharau tawi matunda yanapostawi
    Do not ignore the branch when the fruits on the tree are flourishing
40. Nguo ya kuazima haisitiri matako
    A borrowed garment does not cover one's behind
41. Kupata si kukosa
    Getting something is better than getting nothing
42. Usione kwenda mbele kurudi nyuma si kazi
    You may advance but it is also easy to regress
43. Tamaa mbele mauti nyuma
    When greed is infront of you, death follows
44. Biashara haigombi
    Business has no quarrel
45. Kimya kina maana yake
    Silence has its significance
46. Tabia njema ni silaha yako
    Good behavior is your weapon
47. Kila likuepukalo una kheri nalo
    What abandons you is good riddance
48. Aso bahati habahatishi
    One who is not lucky does not take risks
49. Wapiganapo tembo nyasi huumia
    When elephants fight, the grass gets hurt
50. Ni chombo imara
    It is a strong vessel
51. Nategemea bahati yangu situmaini cha mtu
    I rely on my luck I do not depend on getting something from another person
52. Kinyozi hajinyoi
    A barber does not shave himself
53. Kipatacho nahodha chombo hutua
    A sea vessel settles down when it gets a good captain
54. Sitaki mali nataka radhi
    I do not want wealth. I want consent/blessing
55. Radhi ni bora kuliko mali
    Blessing is better than wealth
56. Likuepukalo ujuwe lina kheri nawe
    What abandons you is good riddance

57. Bahati ikenda kombo mwerevu huwa mjinga
When luck is skewed, an intelligent person becomes unintelligent
58. Hasara ya mtu kukosa akili
Lack of intelligence is a person's loss
59. Aliyeshiba hamjui mwenye njaa
A person who is satiated does not know the one who is hungry
60. Hasira ya mkizi furaha ya mvuvi
The anger of a cuttle fish is a joy to the fisherman/angler
61. Vuta nkuvute yararua nguo
Your pulling and my pulling tears the garment
62. Aliyetota hajui kutota
He who is already submerged (drowned) does not know what drowning is
63. Kwa raha zetu
With our comforts
64. Pesa fitina ya binadamu
Money is man's affliction
65. Utajiri wa moyo ni bora kuliko fedha
A rich (contented) heart is better than wealth
66. Nakiri wangu umaskini siombi wala siazimi
I acknowledge that I am poor, but I neither beg nor borrow
67. Kila mlango kwa ufunguo wake
Each door has its own key

PATIENCE, TOLERANCE AND FAITH
1. Subira ufunguo wa Peponi
Patience is the key to heaven
2. Subiri upate mradi wako
Be patient so that you may get what you want
3. Subira maftah al-kheri
Patience is the key to good
4. Subira ni njema
Patience is good
5. Yailahi nipe moyo wa subira
God give me a patient heart
6. Subira yavuta kheri
Patience brings goodness
7. Jaza yako iko kwa Mungu
Your reward is with God
8. Tulia kwanza
First, calm down
9. Hasira hasara
Anger is regret/loss

10.   Usione namezea ugomvi sikuzoea
       You see me swallowing. I am not used to quarreling
11.   Usishindane na wenye bahati
       Don't compete with the lucky ones
12.   Baada ya dhiki faraji
       Consolation comes after distress
13.   Mpaji ni Mungu
       God is the provider
14.   Sisi sote abiria dereva ni Mungu
       We are all passengers the driver is God
15.   Nakuombea dua
       I am praying for you
16.   Lolote likupatalo limeandikwa na Mungu
       Whatever befalls you, God has ordained it
17.   Imani huwa ni moyoni haiwi mdomoni
       Faith is in the heart not on your lips
18.   Mtaka yote kwa pupa hukosa yote
       He who wants all in haste loses all
19.   Chembe na chembe ni mkate
       A grain and another grain make a loaf
20.   Kinga na kinga ndipo moto huwaka
       A stick and another stick, the fire burns
21.   Kheri kenda shika kama kumi nenda uje
       Holding nine now is better than ten that comes later
22   Raha haiji ila baada ya taabu
       Comfort does not come except after some difficulty
23.   Mwenda pole haumii mguu
       He who walks slowly does not hurt his leg
24.   Ulipendalo hupati hupaata ujaliwalo
       You do not get what you like; you get what God has destined for you
25.   Mungu akupe kheri na mimi nifurahi
       May God give you his blessings and I may be happy
26.   Mungu akupe kila la kheri
       May God give you every thing that is good
27.   Kumezea ni kawaida yangu kwa kuwa sipendi majungu
       My habit is tolerance because I do not like conspiring
28.   Tamu ya Ramadhani ni ibada
       The sweet taste of Ramadhan is worshipping
29.   Mwenye dini hakosi imani
       He who has religion has faith
30.   Imani ya mtu imo ndani ya roho yake
       One's faith is in one's heart
31.   Si madhumuni yangu
       It was not my intention

32. Sitaki raha ya dunia nataka raha ya kesho
    I don't want the comfort of this world. I want the comfort of the next

33. Kilichonyoshwa na Mngu kiumbe hakipeti
    What God has straightened a human being cannot bend

34. Mungu tujalie kheri na baraka tupate tunayotaka
    God give us prosperity and blessings so we may get what we want

35. Ukipata shukuru
    Be grateful when you get something

36. Shukuru na upatacho
    Be grateful of what you get

37. Alitakalo karimu haliwezi mwanadamu
    What God wishes a human being cannot stop

38. Mema na mabaya ndio ulimwengu
    The world is made of good and bad

39. Apendalo Mungu haliwezekani
    No one can undo what God wishes

40. Dua njema kwako mpenzi
    (I am sending) a beautiful prayer for you, my dear

41. Subira huleta mafanikio
    Patience brings success

42. Taratibu ndiyo mwendo
    Slow but sure

43. Mungu muweza
    God has the power

44. Mola tusitiri
    Lord, protect us

45. Mshukuru Mungu kwa kila jambo
    Be grateful to God for everything

46. Kila muomba Mungu hakosi lake fungu
    Every one who prays to God gets his share

47. Upate nia safi kufanikiwa
    To be successful you have to have good intention

48. Imani ninayo bahati sina
    I have faith, but I have no luck

49. Usimsahau mola wako ndiye atowae riziki
    Do not forget your Lord. The one who provides sustenance

50. Mola ndiye mpaji sio mimi wala wewe
    God is the provider, not you nor I

51. Mtupie Mungu kilio sio binaadamu mwenzio
    Address your cry to God not your fellow human being

52. Kusema inshallah si kutekeleza
    Saying God willing is not acting

53. Alyenipa Mola wangu huizuwii riziki yangu
    You cannot stop my sustenance; my Lord has given it to me

54. Usife moyo mwenyezi Mungu yupo
    Don't lose hope there is God

55. Ramadhani in njema tupanyeni [tufanyeni] mema
    The fasting month of Ramadhan is a good month. Let us do what is good

56. Kila mwenye kusubiri mola hatomuadhiri
    God does not disgrace the one who is patient

57. Sundusu ya peponi rabi mola atuvike
    May the Almighty God dress us in heaven's clothes

58. Riziki ni mdudu hutua popote pale
    God's gift is like an insect it lands anywhere

59. Nashukuru kwa yote
    I am grateful for everything

60. Kumcha Mungu ni mwanzo wa hekima
    The fear of God is the beginning of wisdom

61. Kuishi wawili ni kustahamili
    Two people living together requires tolerance

EXPERIENCE, KNOWLEDGE AND ACTION

1. Dunia ni maarifa
   The world is an experience

2. Kuuliza si ujinga
   Asking is not being ignorant

3. Mambo kwa bongo
   Matters require brain

4. Usipoziba ufa utajenga ukuta
   If you do not fill in the crack, you will rebuild the whole wall

5. Utamu wa mchuzi diko-diko kwa pili-pili hoho
   The taste of the curry is from the tiny crushed peppers

6. Jungu kuu halishi koko [ukoko]
   A big cooking pot is never without the burnt bits that stick onto it
   (No one is without blemish)

7. Mkono mtupu haulambwi
   An empty hand is not licked

8. Mkulima mmoja walaji wengi
   One farmer many eaters

9. Wafinyazi hupikia vigae
   Potters usually cook in broken pots

10. Maua huliwa na ndege
    Birds eat flowers

11. Unkula huu
    You have eaten this

12. Kuinamako ndiko kuinukako
    What bends down rises up

13. Ni hivi hivi
    This is how it is

14. Jogoo wa shamba hawiki (haliwiki) mjini
    The country rooster does not crow in town

15. Mchele moja [mmoja] mpishi mwingi. [mapishi mengi]
    There may be one kind of rice but there are different ways of cooking it

16. Liwalo na liwe
    What will be, let it be

17. Mwenye macho haambiwi tizama
    A person who has eyes is not told to look

18. Mti hawendi ila kwa nyenzo
    A log cannot move without the help of rollers

19. Maneno yawe mafupi vitendo viwe virefu
    Let the words be short and actions long

20. Atakae hachoki
    He who wants (something/somebody) does not get tired

21. Padogo pako si pakubwa pa mwenzako
    A small place of your own is better than a bigger one of someone else's

22. Lipitalo hupishwa
    Let bygones be bygones/Let the past go by

23. Fikira nyingi huharibu maarifa
    Too many thoughts ruin the experience

24. Si hoja maneno bora vitendo
    Actions are better than words

25. Vishindo vingi sio kutenda jambo
    Too much commotion is like not acting

26. Afanyaye jambo asilimalize ni kama asiyefanya
    He who does something without finishing it is like the one who does not do

27. Apandae [apandaye] huvuna
    He who plants will harvest

28. Nia yashinda kafara
    Intention defeats a sacrifice to avert wickedness

29. Kawia ufike
    Better late than never

30. Utakuwaje mpishi na wewe waogopa moshi
    How will you be a cook and you are afraid of smoke?

31. Mwangaza mbili moja humponya
    He who looks at two things at once, one of them escapes him.

32. Penye nia pana njia
    Where there is a will there is a way

33. Mchovya asali hachovi mara moja
    He does not taste honey only once (Forbidden fruit is sweet)

34. Kila chombo kwa wimbili
    Every seagoing vessel has its wake
35. Mchagua jembe si mkulima
    A farmer does not choose his tools
36. Ukitaja nyoka shika kigongo
    If you mention a snake, be prepared with a stick (talk of the devil)
37. Mpanda ovyo hula ovyo
    Careless sowing careless harvesting. (As you sow so, you will reep)
38. Macho hayana pazia
    Eyes have no curtain to obstruct them from looking
39. Hayataki nguvu mambo ni ujuzi
    Matters require knowledge not strength
40. Ya leo tamu
    Today's is sweet
41. Usifikirie yaliyopita
    Do not dwell over the past
42. Muungwana hajinadi huonyesha vitendo
    An honorable person does not brag about himself. He acts
43. Mungwana kila aendapo hukumbukwa
    An honorable person is remembered everywhere he goes
44. Kwenda mbio si kufika
    Running is not arriving
45. Udongo wa zamani siyo wa sasa
    Today's clay is not the same as yesterday's
46. Kula kutamu kulima mavune
    Eating is sweet but planting is strainful
47. Mwembamba basi lakini kazi ni ile ile
    He may be thin but the work is the same
48. Gonga gonga usikilze mlio wake
    Knock knock so you may hear the sound
49. Niulize nitakujibu
    Ask me I will answer you
50. Hatari lakini shwari
    Dangerous but calm
51. Fikiri kwanza ndipo uamue
    Think first and then decide
52. Mgaagaa na upwa hali wali mkavu
    He who saunters along the beach never eats plain rice. (He has fish to eat with it)
53. Kuuliza si ujinga
    Asking is not being ignorant
54. Usilolijua litakusumbua
    What you do not know will bother you
55. Shirika haina wema na mla pweke hakuna
    Sharing is not good but no one eats alone

56. Fikiria kabla ujasema [hujasema]
    Think before you speak
57. Nyumba ya maskini haishi kujengwa
    A poor person's house is always under construction
58. Mwenye njaa hana mwiko
    A hungry person does not observe taboo/cannot abstain from food
59. Dunia ni mti mkavu ukiuelemea utakubwaga
    The world is a dry log; if you lean on it, it will break down and drop you
60. Furaha msiba ndio dunia
    The world is made up of happiness and sadness
61. Ukitaka starehe utafute chako
    If you desire comfort, look for what belongs to you
62. Akili ni nywele kila mtu ana zake
    Intelligence is like hair each person has its own kind
63. Jipe moyo utashinda
    Have confidence you will succeed

KINDNESS AND GENEROSITY

1. Hisani haiyozi
   Kindness does not go bad
2. Wema hauozi
   Goodness does not go bad
3. Heri jema
   Good is better
4. Furaha yako faida kwangu
   Your happiness is my gain
5. Furaha yako ni yangu
   Your happiness is mine
6. Haki ya mtu hailiki
   A person's rights cannot be consumed (eaten)
7. Tumkirimu mgeni
   Let us be hospitable to the guest
8. Heri kuzuia kuliko kuuguza
   Prevention is better than cure
9. Kikubwa sina kidogo pokea
   I do not have a big gift. Receive this small one
10. Mla cha mwenziwe na chake huliwa
    He who consumes someone else's property, his gets consumed
11. Wajenga kwa mwenzio(kwa wengine) kwako kwabomoka
    You build for others while your own place is falling down
12. Usikumbuke uovu ukasahau fadhila
    Do not dwell on the bad and forget the kindness

13. Sumu ya mahaba ni nini
     What is the poison of love?

14. Zawadi ni dawa hupoza hasira
     A gift is medicine (a cure). It cools down anger

15. Zawadi ni chochote kupokea usichoke
     Anything is a gift; do not be tired of receiving

16. Naja na heri mwenye nyumba hodi
     Owner of the house, may I come in? I am bringing good fortune

17. Mungu akupe baraka na mie nifurahi
     May God grant you his blessings and I will be happy

18. Mwenyezi Mungu akuzidishie kila la kheri
     May the Almighty God bless you with everything that is good

19. Mwenyezi Mungu akupe baraka na mie nifurahi
     May the Almighty God bless you and I will be happy

20. Nia njema ni tabibu nia mbaya huharibu
     A good intention is a cure, a bad intention is harmful

21. Alozoweya kupokea kutoa ni vita
     He who is used to accepting things for him giving away something is like a war

22. Tenda wema wende zako usingoje shukrani
     Do well and leave. Do not wait for gratitude

23. Ukinipa nitapokea kuiba sikuzoea
     I will accept when you give me. I am not used to stealing

24. Sisemi kitu bali ni furaha moyoni
     I am not saying anything but my heart is happy

25. Hala hala jirani japo ni baniyani
     Be good to a neighbor even if he is a Hindu (of a Banyan caste)

26. Kupendana amani na umoja ni uamuzi
     Love, peace and unity is the decision

27. Mungu akupe furaha na amani maishani
     May God give you happiness and security in your life

28. Mungu akupe kheri daima
     May God give you good fortune always

29. Wema unapandwa wapi nami nikaupaliliye
     Where is goodness planted so I can go and weed it. (look after it?)

30. Hala hala dunia ina meno
     Be ware, the world has teeth

31. Karibuni waungwana nna harusi ya mwana
     Welcome honorable ones. I have my child's wedding

32. Ihsani sina hate [hata] ahsante sipati
     I do not receive kindness nor am I thanked

33. Tunawatakia maisha ya furaha
     We wish you/them a happy life

34. Mwenyezi Mungu akuzidishie kila-la-kheri
     May God increase for you his blessings

35. Alotenda wema hasauliki [hasahauliki]
    One who shows kindness is not forgotten
36. Zawadi menifikia machoni nimeiweka
    I have received your present and I value it
37. Mwenye shukurani hubarikiwa
    The grateful one is blessed
38. Nakuombea wema na baraka
    I pray for your well-being and prosperity
39. Stahili salama idumu daima
    You deserve peace and may it last forever
40. Pokea zawadi ya arusi
    Receive a wedding gift
41. Ukitoa na wakulia [wa kulia] wakushoto [wa kushoto] usijue
    When you give something to someone with your right hand, your left hand
    should not know
42. Ninakuoneya huruma sijui nikwambie
    I feel sorry for you. I do not know whether I should tell you (about something)
43. Ya rabi tupe furaha na sitara
    My Lord give us happiness and protect us
44. Sitosahau fadila [fadhila] kwa dhiki ya mara moja
    I will not forget kindness because of one moment's of distress
45. Utu ni kitendo chema
    Humanity is doing a good deed

IDD GREETINGS

1. Futari ya Ramadhani
   Breakfast for Ramadhan. (The Muslim fasting month)
2. Furaha ya Idd shukuru Mola
   For Idd happiness be thankful to God
3. Eid Mubarak
   Happy Idd
4. Mpenzi wangu pokea mkono wa Iddi
   My dear, accept my Idd greetings
5. Salamu ya Idd kutoka kwa mpenzi wangu
   Idd greetings from my dearest one
6. Asante kwa zawadi ya siku hii ya Iddi
   Thank you for this Idd present
7. Yarabi tupe furaha kwa siku hii ya Iddi
   God grant us happiness on this Idd day
8. Salam ya Idd mpe umpendae
   Give Idd greetings to the one you like/love
9. Pokea Iddi mpenzi upate kunienzi
   Receive this Idd present my dear so, you will think highly of me

10. Mpenzi wangu Eid Mubarak
    My dear, Happy Idd/Eid

11. Pokea zawadi ya Idd uzidi kunienzi
    Receive Idd present so you may think more highly of me

12. Nakuomba iwe Idi ya kheri
    I pray to you (Lord) let it be a good Idd

13. Idd Mubarak mwakani twende Makka
    Idd greetings. Let us go to Mecca next year

14. Tupeane mkono wa Idd kwa furaha na mapenzi yoro [ya roho] mama
    Mother/lady let us exchange heartfelt Idd greetings

15. Ya rabi tupe furaha kwa siku hii ya Idd
    My Lord make us happy on this Idd day

16. Eid mubarak kila mwaka uwe na barka
    Happy Idd. May you be blessed every year/it be a blessed one

17. Barakat il-Idd
    Idd blessings

18. Salama za Idd kutoka (kwa) mpenzi wangu
    Idd's peace from my beloved

19. Mzaa chema Idd Mubarak
    Happy Idd to the mother of a beautiful child

20. Idi nyingi zikufikie neema zake zikufikie
    May you have many Idds. May you be blessed

21. Ya Ilahi tumeona Idd hii na nyingine inshalla
    My Lord, we have seen this Idd and God willing we will see another one

22. Mpenzi wangu eid mubarak kila mwaka uwe na baraka
    Happy Idd my dear. May every year bring blessings

23. Sina cha kukupa nakumbea [nakuombea] dua
    I do not have anything to give you, but you have my prayers

24. Nakuletea mkono wa Idd mola azidishie (akuzidishie) kheri
    I am sending you Idd greetings; may God increase for you his blessings

25. Furaha iwe zaidi siku tukufu za Iddi
    May happiness increase on the Idd holidays

26. Pokea mkono wa Iddi mama
    Mother, receive my Idd greetings

27. Tumeipokea vyema Idd mubarak njema
    We happily welcome the good and blessed Idd

28. Eid mubarak mapenzi yangu na wewe ni ya maisha yetu
    Happy Idd. My love for you is forever

29. Chakukupa sina ila nakuambea [nakuombea] Mungu
    I do not have anything to give you, but I pray for you

30. Bwana hababi Idd said
    My dearest husband happy Idd

31. Ya rabi tujaalie idi ya kheri
    My Lord, give us a happy Idd

32. Karibu idi sikuu [Sikukuu] ya kheri
    Welcome Idd the blessed holiday
33. Muozi mwenzangu mabruk kwa Idd
    My co-in-law, happy Idd
34. Karibu Idi siku yenye kheri
    Welcome Idd a day of blessings
35. Pokea habibi zawadi ya idi
    My dearest, receive an Idd gift
36. Hongera ya Idd mubarak
    Congratulations on a happy Idd
37. Umenifurahisha hadi kunikumbuka siku ya Idd
    You have made me happy by remembering me on Idd day
38. Ewe Mola wetu na iwe sherehe ya furaha kwetu
    O our Lord, make it a happy celebration for us
39. Hija mbruran. [mabrura]
    May God accept your pilgrimage to Mecca
40. Pokea eid mola atujaliye tupendane milele
    Receive Idd greetings and may God grant us ever-lasting love

POLITICS AND NATIONAL IDENTITY

1. Faida ya wananchi kuijenga nchi
   It is for the benefit of the citizens to build the country
2. Uishi wapi
   Where should you live?
3. Uno na uno nitunde upi
   This one and that one, which place (political party) do I choose?
4. Burudika moyo wako ujenge taifa lako
   Cool down your heart and build your nation
5. Hapo ni kwako
   That place is your home
6. Omani amani
   Oman is peaceful
7. 'Umaan aSliy wa faSliy
   Oman is my origin and my family
8. 'Uman alyawm
   Today's Oman
9. Amiyrat ul-baHar
   The Sea Princess
10. Masiyna raswat Salaala
    Masira is Salala's haven
11. Twalipenda Azimio la Arusha
    We like the Arusha Declaration

12. Tusisahau kwetu
     Let us not forget our home
13. Sikizana na wenzio ujenge ujamaa
     Get along with your friends in order to build familyhood (African socialism)
14. Salama salimina
     Safe and sound
15. Kupendana amani na umoja
     Love, peace and unity
16. Saba Saba ya ishirini na mbili, 1976 Tanzania
     The twenty-second anniversary of TANU (Tanganyika African National Union)
17. Kinasema chama chetu kilimo msingi wetu
     Our party says farming is our foundation
18. Utekelezaji ndio wajibu wetu kuijenga nchi yetu
     Fulfillment is our duty to build our country
19. ArDuna aTTayyiba 'aashat 'Uman
     Our beautiful land. Long live Oman
20. Uchumi wa nchi ndio maendeleo yetu
     The country's earnings/economy is our progress
21. Azimio la Arusha
     Arusha Declaration
22. Wengi wape usipowapa watachukua kwa mikono yao
     Give to the majority. If you don't give them, they will take with their own hands
23. Watanzania tumuenzi baba wa taifa
     Tanzanians let us honor the father of the nation
24. Muokoa nchi ndio mwananchi
     The citizen is the one who saves the country

KANGA NAMES AND THEIR DISTRIBUTION

Category	Proverb (Familiar)	Proverb (New)	Speech form	Total
Friendship	18	95	80	193
Hostility	20	100	44	164
Family	13	40	40	93
Wealth	18	25	24	67
Patience	9	19	33	61
Experience	27	29	7	63
Kindness	13	17	15	45
Idd Greetings	0	6	34	40
Politics & Identity	0	15	9	24

Map

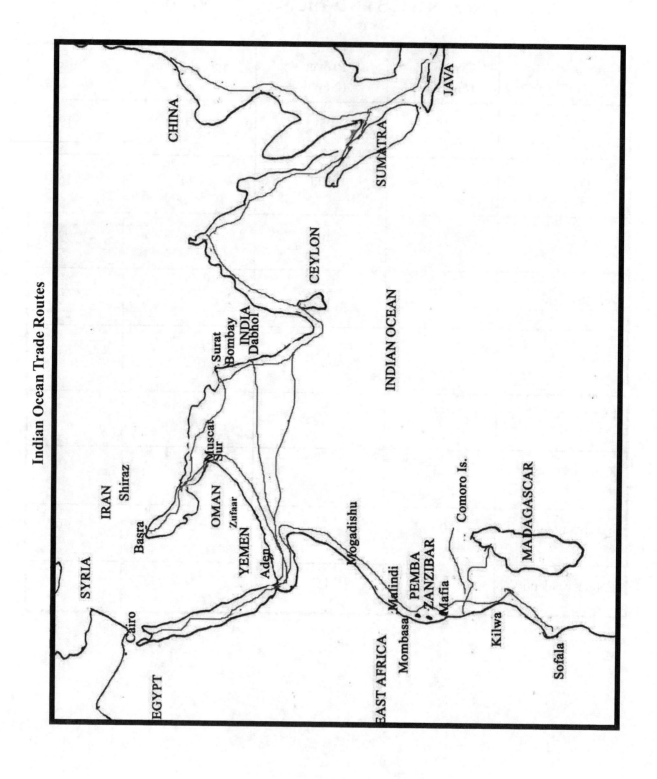

REFERENCES

Abdillah, Farouque and Gill Shapherd, "I am like a kanga-cloth. I die in all my beauty" *Africa Now*, February 1984.

Abdullah, Fatma Shaaban, "Reflections on a symbol." *Africa Now* (February1984): 49-51.

Al-Idris, Abi'Abdallah MuHammad bin MuHammad 'Abdallah bin Hasan, *Kitaab Nuzhat al-Mushtaaq fiy Ikhtiraaq al-afaaf* [The recreation of he who yearns to traverse the lands] Roma, 1977.

Al-Masùdi, Ibn al-Husayn, Kitab Al-Dhahab wa Maàdinu al-Jawhar, Cairo, 1300.

Alley, Mahfoudha, *"The Power of Kanga"*, The City, Mombasa, Kenya, n.d.13.

Barbosa, Duarte, *A Description of the Coasts of East Africa and Malabar in the Beginning of the 16*[th] *Century* (Translated by Henry J. Stanley) London, The Hakluyt Society, 1866.

Beck, Rose-Marie, "Aesthetics of Communication: Texts and Textiles (Leso) from the East African Coast (Swahili)," *Research in African Literatures*, 31, 3 (Winter 2000) 104-124.

————, "Ambiguous Signs: The Role of the Kanga as a Medium of Communication", *Swahili Forum* VIII, 2001,157-169.

Browne, J.Ross, *Etchings of a Whaling Cruise*, New York, 1846.

Burton, Richard F., *Zanzibar, City, Island and Coast*, Vol. I, London,1872.

————, *The Lake Regions of Central Africa*, London, 1860.

Chittick, H.Neville, in "The Shirazi Colonization of East African Coast", London, 1965.

Craster, J.E.E., *Pemba, The Spice Island of Zanzibar*, London, 1913.

Fair, Laura, "Dressing Up: Clothing, Class and Gender in Post-Abolition Zanzibar" *Journal of African History*, 39,1998, 63-94.

————, *Past Times and Politics, Ohio University Press*.2001.

Fitzgerald, W.W.A, *Travels in British East Africa Zanzibar and Pemba*, London, 1898.

Graebner, Werner, (ed.), *Sokomo Popular Culture in East Africa* Amsterdam, 1992, 67.

Gray, Sir John, *History of Zanzibzr from the Middle Ages to 1856*, London,1962.

Hanby, Jeanette and David Bygott, *Kangas:101 uses*, Nairobi, 1985.

Hilgar, J. 1995, "The Kangas: An example of East African Textile design" in J.Picton (ed.) *The Art of African Textiles*, 44 - 45.

Hofman,Rachel , "Islamic symbols in secular contexts: The Fulani kerka" unpublished paper.

Ibn BaTTuTa, Abu Abdullah Muhammad Ibn Ibrahim, *RiHlat, TuHfat al-NuZZar fiy Gharaaib al-amSaar wa 'ajaaib al-asfaar-* [The Wonders of Cities and the Marvels of Travels.] Bairut, 1964.

Ingrams, Harold, *Arabia and the Isles*, London, 1919.

Johnson, F., *A Standard Swahili-English Dictionar* , London, 1939.

Krapf, Johannes Ludwig, *Vocabulary of Six East African Languages*, London,1850

————, *A Dictionary of the Swahili Language*, London, 1882.

Krumm, Bernhard, *Words of Oriental Origin in Swahili*, London, 1940.

Lyne, Robert Nunez, *Zanzibar in Contemporary Times*, London, 1905.

Mirza, Sara. and Strobel M., *Three Swahili Women Life*, Indiana, 1989.

New, Charles, *Life Wanderings and Labours in Eastern Africa*, London, 1873.

Nicholls,C.S., 1971, *The Swahili Coast*, London, 1971.

Owen, W.F.W., *Narratives to explore the shores of Africa and Arabia*, Vol. I and II, New York, 1833.

Pearce, F.B., *The Island Metropolis of Eastern Africa*, London, 1920.

Picton, John and John Mack, (eds.) *The Art of African Textiles*, Place, 1995.

Rechenbach, Charles, *Swahili-English Dictionary*,Washington, 1967.

Renne, Elisha. P, *Cloth That Does Not Die,* Seattle and London, 1995.

Robert, Shaaban, *Siti Bint Saad,* Dar es Salaam, 1961.

Salt, Henry, *Voyage to Abyssinia*, Philadelphia, 1816.

Smee, *Voyage to the Eastern Shores of Africa,* Vol. VI, Transactions of the Bombay Geographical Society, London, 1844.

Steere, Edward, *Swahili Tales*, London, 1870,

————, *A Handbook of the Swahili Language as Spoken in Zanzibar*, London, 1875.

Yahya-Othman, "If Cap Fits: Kanga Names and Women's Voice in Swahili Society," *Swahili Forum* IV, Koln,1997,135-50.

Younghusband, Ethel, *Glimpses of East Africa and Zanzibar,* London, 1908.

Velten, C., *Prosa und Poesie der Suaheli*, Berlin, 1907.

Vincent, William, *The Periplus of the Erythrean Sea*, London, 1800.

Zawawi, Sharifa, 1998, *African Muslim Names: Images and Identities*, N.J.,1998.

————, *Loan Words and their Effect on the Classification of Swahili Nominals,* Leiden, 1979.

————, *Jifunze Kiswahili Chetu,* N.J., 1990.

Indexes

INDEX OF PROPER NAMES

A
Abdillahi, Farouque, xi, 125
Abdullah, Fatma Shaaban, 15, 18-19, 21, 26, 125
Al-Idris, 5-6, 17, 85, 125
Alley, Mahfoudha H., 22, 26, 125
Al-Masùdi, 3, 125
Alpers, Edward, 3, 17
Avezard, Claude, 30

B
Barbosa, Duarte, 6-7, 17, 29, 85, 125
Beck, Rose Marie, x, xii, 17-18, 125
Blok, H.P., viii, xi, 125
Burton, R.F., 1-2, 4, 9-10, 12, 14, 17-18, 29, 85, 125
Buttner, Carl G., 18

C
Craster, J. E. E., 17-18, 125
Chittick, H. Neville, 2-4, 125

F
Fair, Laura, xi, 22, 26, 125
Fitzgerald, W. W., 30, 125

G
Gray, Sir John, xi, 125

H
Hilgar, J., xi-xii, 17, 26, 125
Hanby, Jeannette and Pygott, David, x, 82, 84, 125
Hourani, George Fadlo, 2, 4, 125
Hussein, Ebrahim, 75

I
Ibn-BaTTuTa, 6, 17, 30, 85, 125
Ingrams, Harold, viii, xi, 125

J
Johnson, Frederick, 1-2, 4, 9-11, 17-18, 26, 125

K
Krapf, J. Ludwig, 11-13, 15-16, 18, 29, 125
Krumm, Bernhard, viii, xi, 18, 125

M
Meinhof, M., viii
Mirza, Sara and Strobel M., 30, 125
New, Charles, 13-14, 18, 125
Nyerere, Julius, vi, 21, 62

O
Owen, W.F.P., viii, xii, 8, 13, 17, 29-30, 85, 125

P
Pearce, F.B., 1, 4, 125

S
Saad, Siti Bint, 81, 84, 125
Salt, Henry, 8, 126
Sengo, T.S. , 78, 84
Shepherd, Gill , xi
Steere, Edward, 11-12, 14-16, 18, 85, 126

V
Velten, Carl, 16, 18, 126
Vincent, William, iii, 4, 126

Y
Yahya-Othman, xii, 126
Younghusband, Ethel, 16, 24, 26, 126

Z
Zawawi, Sharifa, 4, 18, 26

GENERAL INDEX

C
Cloth, vii-xii, 2, 4, 5-18, 23, 28-29, 31, 77, 82-83, 85-86, 125
  doti, 5, 9-11, 13, 15-16, 18-19, 82
  garments, x, 3, 5-6, 9-11, 3, 16-17, 31, 82
  kaniki, 9-11, 14
  kisutu/kisuto, vi, 5, 9, 11-16, 61, 85
  leso, vii-viii, 5, 9-11, 13, 15-18, 28-29, 82, 85, 125
  merkani, 9-10
  nguo- nguo mbili (two pieces of cloth), ix, 5, 7, 9-13, 15-17, 19, 26, 35, 42, 46, 82, 85, 94, 110-111
  shuka (loin cloth), 7, 10-11, 13-14, 27, 85
Cotton plantations, 30
  Economy, 20, 29, 60, 122
  manufacture, 8-9, 10, 23, 29
  marketing, 16
  production, 19, 29-30
  weaving, 11

F
Festivals, Islamic
  Idd, xi-xii, 33, 57-58, 76, 87, 106-107, 119-121, 123
  Nairuz/Mwaka, vi, 2, 28, 65,
Flags, 20

I
Indian Ocean trade routes, 124
Innovations, 82-84
  bilingual name, 83
  kanga bubu (lacking messages) , vi, xi, 25, 30, 40, 67-68, 82
  roman script/letters, 21-23, 32, 82

K

Kanga, iii, vi-xii, 2-88, 90, 92, 94, 120, 122-123, 125-126
colors, 11, 14-15, 19-21, 23, 25, 30, 83
designs, vii, 3, 10, 15-17, 19-21, 23, 26, 50, 57, 83
fashions, 19-26
good taste, 10, 24
names, 31, 39, 77, 83, 86-87, 123, 126
names in Arabic script, vi, 7, 17, 20-22, 61, 82-83
names in Roman script, 22-23, 32, 82
with names, 9-10, 82
without names, 40, 83

L

Languages, 13, 18, 43, 83, 125
Arabic, 2-4, 7, 9-11, 13, 16-18, 20-23, 26, 40, 48, 75, 63, 81-83, 85, 93
English, ix-x, 7-8, 10-11, 24, 29, 83, 85, 100
Kiswahili, ix, 3, 17, 26, 126
Literature, vii-viii, x, 5, 15, 24, 77-81, 125
metaphors, 86
new proverbs, 79-80
oral tradition, vii, ix, 24, 26, 32
proverbs, 22, 75-80, 84
rhymes, ix, 28, 80-81
riddle, 15, 31, 102, 103
sayings, 30-31, 42, 44, 47, 50-53, 55-56, 60, 77, 80-82
songs, ix, 28, 80-81

M

Messages on kangas, vii, ix, x-xi 4, 22-25, 31-60, 75-76
action, xi, 33-34, 52-53, 87, 103, 114
children's, ix, 5, 16, 27-28, 43, 105

cooperation and competition, xi, 32, 44
divorce, 36-37, 44, 75
experience and knowledge, xi, 33, 52-54, 75, 87, 114-123
faith, xi, 33, 37, 49, 51-52, 87, 112-113
familial relationships, xi, 32, 99
friendship, xi, 32-35, 80, 82, 87-88, 90, 123
hostility and resentment, xi, 32, 37-40, 87
kindness and generosity, xi, 33, 55, 87
love, xi, 31-39, 43-45, 47, 57-58, 60, 80, 82-83, 87-97, 99, 103, 105-107, 118-122
marriage, xi, 18, 25, 27, 32-33, 35-39, 52, 75, 87, 93, 108
mother, viii, 25-27, 40-42, 44, 75, 85, 98, 101, 104-108, 120
men's, 24, 86
parents, 32, 40, 42-44, 82, 105-107
patience and tolerance, 48-53, 111-114, 123
wealth and strength, xi, 8, 20, 22, 32, 40, 44-48, 81, 86
women's, 12, 14, 16, 31, 86, 126
Missionary, 11, 29
Movements of people, 3
contact, ix, 1-3, 7, 13, 17, 25, 85
diasporas, xi, 86
trade, viii, 2-3, 6-9, 13, 16-17, 29, 82-83, 85
Wamanga, 1-2
Waswahili, 1, 3, 5, 7, 9, 11, 13-15, 17, 23, 26-27, 31-32, 35, 38, 45, 75, 82, 85-86
Myths, vii-viii

P

Politics, xi, 29, 33, 59, 75, 87, 121, 123, 125
commemorative, 21, 15, 59, 75, 83
development, viii-ix, xi, 32, 75, 86
identity, xi, 3, 33, 59, 86-87, 121, 123
nationality, xi, 59, 75, 121-122
parties, 21

V

Values, vii, ix, xi, 3, 31-32, 48-49, 51, 57, 84-86
culture, viii, xi, 1, 3, 7, 13, 31, 40, 84, 86, 125
discourse, 48, 80-81, 83-84, 86
education, 21-22, 28
ethics, xi
moral, xi, 77
upbringing, 43-44, 107